"This is a book I didn't eve ly weaves the human experience o al Family Systems model. The result is a deeply healing work that gives voice to, and hope for, the journey so many of us are on."

— **Lizz Enns Petters**, co-host of the *Deconstructing Mamas* podcast

"There couldn't be better timing for this book to be published. With so many of us completely disconnected from our inner family, not knowing how to dive deeper into understanding how this disconnection plays out in our everyday life, this book offers wisdom, practical insights and much-needed hope for us to reconnect and embrace our True Self. Molly knocks it out of the park!"

— **Esther Joy Goetz**, co-host of the *Deconstructing Mamas* podcast and author of *Wit, Wisdom and Whimsy*

JOURNEY TO SHALOM

Finding Healing, Wholeness, and Freedom In Sacred Stories

Molly LaCroix, LMFT

Journey To Shalom: Finding Healing, Wholeness, and Freedom In Sacred Stories

ISBN: 979-8-218-29858-6

Also available as an ebook and audiobook.

Cover design: Karla Colahan - The Inspired Foundry
Interior layout: Jonathan Puddle

For my mother
whose courage to embrace change
in every season of life
inspires me.

Contents

Preface

Welcome. You've been on my mind and heart as I crafted this manuscript—which I hope will be a resource that supports your healing and faith journey.

They are connected, aren't they—healing and faith? We reach out to God to make sense of suffering, and to connect with a compassionate presence when we feel alone, hopeless, or overwhelmed. Faith spurs us to turn toward God, whose company we hope can sustain us as we work to heal from life's wounds.

That's the ideal, anyway.

Perhaps that hasn't been your experience. In my work as a therapist, I've heard stories from clients who turned to their spiritual communities for support, and failed to find God's loving presence in people who reacted to their struggles with judgment, legalism, advice, or "correct" beliefs. When we reach out for connection, we often encounter barriers.

Stories of faith leaders who abuse their power and platforms to harm people compound our disappointment. There are those who wield Scripture as a weapon and a wall rather than a guide to restoration and reconciliation. We may wonder why Christians talk so much about love but often fail to be loving. I wrote my first book, *Restoring Relationship: Transforming Fear into Love Through Connection,* to address that very issue.

I have also observed that in our frustration and discouragement with the failures of our faith communities, it is tempting to close the Bible and give up on its sacred stories. When spiritual tools have left us high and dry, many seek healing only through secular models offered by therapists.

But what if we can have the best of both worlds?

I have witnessed the power of integrating healthy Christian spirituality with secular models that address the root cause of individual and relational challenges. And I've seen the impact in my own life. I've learned how sacred stories in Scripture connect with our own sacred stories—the stories we hold that deserve our reverent attention. Connecting with our stories is transformative.

Transformation is not a hyper-spiritual ideal attainable only by a few "holy" people. Jesus' vision for his ministry tells us otherwise: "The Spirit of the Lord is on me, because he has anointed me to preach good news to the poor. He has sent me to proclaim freedom for the prisoners and recovery of sight for the blind, to release the oppressed, to proclaim the year of the Lord's favor."[1] The Spirit longs to free all of us from oppression—from the things that constrain our thriving.

You may wonder about the possibility of deep healing. You may have tried different methods, but encountered persistent challenges that have cast doubt. I understand your potential skepticism, and I welcome it. I invite you to bring your full self, with your doubts and fears, as you explore these pages. If you can approach this with curiosity, you may find a fresh perspective on some ancient truths and practices that I believe will restore your hope.

The model I will present is congruent with the overarching story of Scripture, and is also consistent with what we're learning about humanity through neuroscience and psychotherapy. I believe the confluence of Scripture and science offers the best hope for healing and transforming deep wounds.

Scripture repeatedly tells the story of intimacy marred by brokenness, followed by exile, then redemption and restoration through a loving relationship. This is the story of God's people, and it is my story too. I believe you'll discover it is your story as well.

I don't know the depth of your pain or how you adapted to the adversity you experienced. However, I do know—because it is the human condition—that you carry pain, and that parts of you work diligently to control or contain that pain. Be assured, though, no matter what you've experienced, your complex and nuanced story also includes beauty and goodness.

I want to invite you to connect more deeply with your story and the characters who make you the unique and wonderful person God created. I want you to love yourself—all of who you are—unconditionally, as God loves you. And through loving all of who you are—including vulnerable and protective parts within—you will heal. I want for you to return from the exile of loneliness and pain to a restored sense of intimacy with yourself, others, and God.

---

1. Luke 4:18-19, NIV

I invite you to join me in pursuing your heart's goals. They are attainable. The Great Commandment—to love God and one another as we love ourselves—describes a state of harmonious relational existence that the ancient Hebrews called *shalom.* More than simply peace—however precious peace is—*shalom* means wholeness. Jesus announced a ministry dedicated to freeing the oppressed to motivate us to journey with him toward freedom and wholeness. Brennan Manning quotes a friend's definition of wholeness that speaks to my hope for you: "Wholeness is brokenness owned and thereby healed."[2] The Great Commandment is much more than words to live by; it is a vision of wholeness through mutually loving relationships. It guides our journey.

We all need a roadmap for our travels, along with practices that support our transformation. This book relies on a transformative psychotherapy model called Internal Family Systems (IFS), which I illustrate through Bible stories that illuminate crucial information about human functioning and the process of healing. Theologian and pastor Greg Boyd notes, "If our faith is going to be powerful and transformative, it is going to have to be imaginative and experiential."[3] Spiritual practices that are both imaginative and experiential follow each chapter so that you can explore each step of the process yourself.

We sometimes think of spiritual practices in traditional terms, such as prayer, worship, or service. But Rabbi Danya Ruttenberg writes, "I define a spiritual practice as an ongoing, repeated activity that, when performed with intentionality, can transform how we understand ourselves, others, the world around us—and our connection to the sacred...or God."[4] Spiritual practices help us shift from a purely cognitive engagement with information to an embodied experience, which is crucial for healing.

You might wonder how biblical texts can illustrate a secular psychotherapy model. It is not as far-fetched as it might seem. Biblical scholar R.W.L. Moberly notes the approach of "the writers of the great Old Testament narratives and of the Gospels...is closer to the approach of the historical novelist or dramatist, with a

---

2. *Abba's Child: The Cry of the Heart for Intimate Belonging,* Brennan Manning, pg. 55

3. Gregory Boyd, https://reknew.org/2022/06/why-your-imagination-matters/, retrieved 6/7/22

4. Rabbi Danya Ruttenberg newsletter 6/19/23

concern to speak to the present through creative use of the past."[5] I am excited for you to see your own story and your present circumstances in a fresh way through ancient stories and modern psychology.

I believe you will see the echo of your journey in the arc of Scripture: from intimacy to brokenness and exile to restoration, redemption, and reconciliation—the journey to *shalom*.

---

5. *The Bible in a Disenchanted Age: The Enduring Possibility of the Christian Faith*, R.W.L. Moberly, pg. 5

Chapter One

Journey to Shalom

Luke 8:40-48

Over the years, Rachel watched as her sisters, cousins, and friends married and had children.[1] They effortlessly and naturally filled roles celebrated for women, while she stood at a distance weighed down by despair over a body society deemed worthless and even dangerous.

Rachel typically made an effort to avoid family gatherings, but sometimes she couldn't resist drawing near to see loved ones and hear the chattering of playful children. The ache in her heart was so intense she could only watch for a few moments before turning away. Tears running down her cheeks, she retreated to her home on the outskirts of the village, carefully placed where no one would be contaminated by her.

There were brief moments of hope when Rachel thought someone might violate the strict rules; the longing for a hug filled her with an overwhelming urge to run toward a loved one when they crossed paths in the village. But, before she could act on her impulse, they would turn away, eyes filled with pity, leaving her alone with her shame.

"You are so stupid!" said an inner voice. "After all these years, you should know better! No one is going to hug you. No one cares what you need. So stop hoping, and accept that this is God's will."

After all, she had tried so many remedies, and no one could heal her. In time, a protective part of her told her to minimize her needs so she might get through the day without feeling the pain of hopelessness, shame, or despair. Numbness wasn't living, but it had its benefits.

---

1. The bleeding woman in this story is anonymous. I chose to name her "Rachel" because Jesus calls her "daughter" and the Hebrew name "Rachel" means female sheep. Jesus welcomed her into his flock, his family.

Still, as Rachel lay in the dark, she dared to cry out to God, to believe healing was possible. Despite years of suffering, she sometimes felt the warmth of God's presence in quiet moments and heard a whisper, "You are my beloved child." In her desperation, she nurtured the spark of hope that her life mattered.

How she longed to believe she was beloved! But brief moments of confidence usually gave way to doubt. Rachel was tired of the toll her conflicting emotions took. It felt easier to accept that God would never heal her.

Then Rachel began to hear stories about a teacher named Jesus who was traveling around healing people. Wherever he went, crowds followed and miracles happened. When she learned that women healed from evil spirits and diseases were funding his ministry and traveling with him, hope welled up. Deep inside, Rachel felt a frisson of confidence that she, too, could be healed.

A few days later when Rachel went to the well for water she heard an excited buzzing among the other women. "Jesus is coming!" said one of them. Within minutes, people were pouring out of their homes and gathering along the road.

A voice inside her warned Rachel not to take a risk or violate the rules by entering a crowd who could turn and heap more shame on her, but courage she didn't know she possessed welled up, and she began to move toward the crowd waiting for Jesus.

As she neared the people, she saw the synagogue leader fall at Jesus' feet, begging him to heal his dying daughter. Surely Jesus would leave their village to tend to her. Disappointment welled up, threatening to block the courage propelling her toward Jesus. She felt the tug and pull of conflicting inner voices.

"Why would he stop for you?" the critical voice said. "You're someone God has cursed."

"There must be some reason you don't deserve healing, and this is just more proof. Turn back before you humiliate yourself," said the doubting voice.

But, when Rachel looked at the women walking with Jesus, the confidence that she was worthy of healing bubbled up, and she moved toward him. Her heart was racing and she could barely breathe.

A gentle voice inside said, "Just touch his cloak."

The love she felt accompany that voice propelled her last few steps. She reached out, her head down so no one would recognize her, and the tip of her finger grazed the edge of Jesus' cloak.

In that instant, the ache in her womb dissipated. For a moment, Rachel felt peace. The critical inner voice was silent, her despair and hopelessness replaced by the warmth of loving-kindness.

Then Jesus asked, "Who touched me?"[2]

Fear rushed in. The part of her who spent years abiding by strict rules was terrified that she would be shamed.

She walked a few steps and fell at Jesus' feet, her face inches from the dirt. She took a breath, knowing that this moment would determine her future. Either she would be banished for good, left to wander in the desert until she lay down to die, or she would be restored.

The love radiating from Jesus gave her the energy to speak, to share her story. "I touched the edge of your cloak, and I was healed."

She heard the most loving words imaginable. "Daughter, your faith has healed you. Go in peace."[3]

Hope for Healing

Go in peace. Return to wholeness, to belonging, to *shalom*.

The faith that love matters most, more than the consistency of rules or the safety of minimizing needs and staying small, energized the bleeding woman, allowing her to risk reaching out for healing.

Have you wondered if you'll ever heal? If real and lasting change is possible? Can the critical voice, the anxiety that takes over your body, or the shame lurking deep in your soul really be loved into wholeness?

Maybe you, too, try to follow all of your family or spiritual community's rules. You put others' needs and comfort first, often losing track of your own needs. You know how to get through the day, to show up and fulfill responsibilities, but your body feels weighed down by frustration and, sometimes, despair. Is wholeness, *shalom,* really possible?

The stories in Scripture contain more than history or theology. They reveal humanity at its best and worst, mirroring our deepest wounds and the questions they provoke.

---

2. Luke 8:45, NIV

3. Luke 8:48, NIV

The people we encounter in the Bible are not characters or caricatures; they are humans who feel the same emotions and want the same things we do: love, safety, connection, and purpose. They grapple with our questions, especially the ultimate question of where God is when we suffer. If God "is love",[4] how is Love present in our particular circumstances?

Can we trust that God cares deeply about healing?

The story of the bleeding woman is an example of someone imprisoned and oppressed by her legalistic spiritual community who is set free by faith and grace. In it, we see the healing power of love, curing her physical ailment and also releasing the grip of her inner critic and the parts of her who tried to manage her distress by minimizing pain and discounting her needs.

God's love lifted the burdens from tender parts of her who held grief, despair, shame, and a sense of unworthiness. True healing, lasting change, happens when Love reaches all parts of us and frees us from the burdens life has shackled us with and the many ways we adapt to survive.

Entering stories like hers can help us enter our own; sacred stories serve as a bridge into our inner worlds where pain, protective strategies, and the resources we possess as bearers of God's image reside. I believe her story of healing can be your story too.

The healing journey of any human, ancient or current, is not linear, and the stories preserved in Scripture are rarely neat and tidy. And that is their power. They are stories of real people, people whose struggles will validate your pain. While some church folks may gloss over your suffering and offer frustrating platitudes, the people whose stories populate Scripture never do. Their stories will show you that the ways you've learned to adapt to pain are universal. By entering their stories, you may find a deep connection to the community of people who have persevered in a life of faith for thousands of years, clinging to the hope of redemption and allowing God to meet their most profound needs.

The model I will unpack will show you how God's gentle love can bring healing and wholeness to every tender, vulnerable part of you.

---

4. 1 John 4:8 NIV

A New Way of Understanding Ourselves

The psychotherapy model I use in my work, Internal Family Systems (IFS), provides a method for entering stories—others' and our own—that facilitates healing. While there is value in feeling an emotional connection with someone as they tell their story, far more is involved for the story to become a vehicle for healing. The first step is adopting a new way of understanding ourselves.

The foundational concept of IFS is that we are multiple, containing a variety of parts or subpersonalities. While this may be a new concept for some, I suspect you've once said or felt something like, "A part of me wants to quit my job and work for myself, but another part is afraid of losing financial security." Different inner voices and conflicting emotions often emerge whenever we face a decision, especially a difficult one.

Sadly, too often, multiplicity is feared, misunderstood, or even pathologized. Yet multiplicity is inherent in Creation, an aspect of God's creative design readily manifest in atoms (protons, neutrons, electrons), human families, and ecological systems. These systems function because each element contributes to the whole. All of Creation is *relational.* The Triune God created a world with *inter*dependence—where healthy functioning requires healthy relationships.

The developer of IFS, Dr. Richard Schwartz, was trained in systems theories that explained family dynamics and helped individuals and families heal. He realized that dynamics (patterns of interaction) common to families explained what clients reported about their internal world.[5] When he decided to "listen carefully and trust what [his] clients were telling [him] about their inner worlds,"[6] he noticed clients routinely referred to "parts" of themselves with a wide variety of feelings, thoughts, and behaviors.[7] Clients felt distinct differences between parts like young children, others who were fierce taskmasters, and some who would resort to extreme behaviors such as self-harm when the client was flooded by pain.

---

5. *Internal Family Systems Therapy (2nd ed.)*, Richard C. Schwartz and Martha Sweezy, pg.15

6. Ibid, pg. 13

6. Ibid, pg. 13

7. Ibid, pg. 12

These disparate parts were sometimes aligned with one another and sometimes in conflict, just as members of families have alliances and conflicts.[8]

It became apparent to Dr. Schwartz that multiplicity is the normal human condition and, more importantly, developing loving relationships with the different parts of ourselves facilitates healing. That was the birth of the Internal Family Systems model.

The Internal Family Systems (IFS) Model

As the name implies, the family analogy helps us understand the different parts of ourselves, our "internal family members." Rather than disconnected thoughts, emotions, sensations, and images, the content of our minds and bodies reflects the presence of a variety of internal family members or "parts" of ourselves. For example, the Apostle Paul's well-known lament illustrates the presence of different internal family members: "I do not understand what I do. For what I want to do I do not do, but what I hate I do."[9] One part of Paul wanted to be compliant, another part resisted, and a third criticized him for the conflict!

If you wonder whether you can relate to this verse, try setting an intention. For example, when you desire to eat less sugar, exercise more, or work less, you may notice a polarity, a tug-of-war between parts of you with different opinions. If you attend to your inner experience, you might notice an emotion, such as doubt, accompanied by a thought, "I don't trust myself to keep this commitment," and associated tension somewhere in your body. Like falling dominoes, the presence of one part often brings awareness of others. Your doubter is challenged by a frustrated part, saying, "What's wrong with you? You're so weak! Why can't you stick to your commitments?!" Your stomach might tighten and your shoulders knot up as your inner critic joins the conversation.

Perhaps this is resonating, but you wonder whether the model is congruent with Scripture. God created humans as biological, psychological, social, emotional, and spiritual beings—a system with multiple elements. We learn God's truth in various ways, including through Scripture and observing human functioning. The more I have studied, experienced, and worked with this

---

8. Ibid, pg. 13

9. Romans 7:15

model, the more I have seen that it is profoundly biblical. The metanarrative of Scripture—creation, brokenness, exile, redemption, restoration—is a story of hope for healing. Therefore, a secular psychotherapy model that provides both a way of understanding ourselves and a process for healing—freeing people from dysfunctional behaviors and relationships and restoring wholeness—*is* congruent with Scripture.

The Leader of the Internal Family

One of Dr. Schwartz's most compelling discoveries is the most profoundly biblical aspect of the model. As he worked with clients, helping them connect with internal family members who played differing roles, the various parts of them would ultimately relax. Then, clients exhibited qualities such as compassion, clarity, and confidence. When Dr. Schwartz asked which part that was, they said something like, "That's not a part like those other voices; that's who I really am, that's my *self*."[10] Over time, Dr. Schwartz found no matter what a client experienced in life, no matter how extreme their trauma or wounding, a leader in the internal family—simply called "Self"—existed, which possessed resources he describes as the eight "Cs:" compassion, curiosity, clarity, courage, calm, confidence, creativity, and connection.[11]

These qualities are inherent in every human being; they are not a developmental outcome or the result of training.[12] They are present from birth, and adversity cannot damage them. They are God's image in us.[13]

We are created in the image of God, who "is love."[14] Consider how each of these qualities reflects love. Different situations require love in various forms. When we first meet another person, *curiosity* expresses love. If there's injustice, love looks like *courage*, fueling actions to right a wrong. Relationship challenges often require

10. Ibid, pg. 17

11. Ibid, pg. 49-53

12. Ibid, pg. 276

13. Genesis 1:26-27, NIV

14. 1 John 4:8, NIV

both *creativity* and *clarity* as we navigate decisions about boundaries. When the Self—the image of God in us—leads the internal family, love flows internally and externally in myriad forms.

I will sometimes use the term "Self-energy" as we continue this journey. God's love—in all of its forms—is *energy*, a power that enables something to work, happen or change. Think of how your body feels in the presence of one of your favorite people. You can often feel the flow of love in your body; it is life's most potent energy force.

Nothing can damage God's image within us. A gift of grace, the Self, the leader of the internal family, possesses the resources needed for healing. All high-functioning families have effective leadership. As bearers of God's image, we have many qualities of capable leaders. It bears repeating these are intrinsic resources present in each individual, no matter their life circumstances. You can learn to access all of these qualities to support your healing. They are not a developmental outcome; you possess them inately from birth because you bear God's image; you just might need a little guidance to identify them.

Your journey to wholeness is the same as your journey of sanctification, where you lead your inner family away from bondage and into freedom, by drawing on the resources God has given you, creating a loving community that reflects God's image.

The Impact of Adversity on the Internal Family

All this may sound lovely, but I'm guessing you're starting to think I'm describing a fantasy. Where were these resources the last time you struggled in a relationship, were flooded with shame, or felt overwhelmed by symptoms of anxiety or depression? In situations that feel challenging, you suffer the impact of life experiences on your inner family. No one escapes adversity. Your story has chapters containing events that left burdens in your system, burdens that block or constrain the God-given resources needed for abundant living—and healing.

Burdens of intense emotions such as shame, distorted beliefs such as "I am worthless," uncomfortable sensations, and distressing images stick to our minds and lodge in our bodies. Members of the internal family who experienced adversity carry these burdens. These parts of us are vulnerable, and their burdens pose a risk to the rest of the inner family. If the pain they hold surfaces, it can derail our functioning.

These burdened parts become "*exiles*" in the internal family—cast out because of the threat posed by their wounds. Imagine them locked in the basement of the family home.

Exiles: The Vulnerable Members of the Internal Family

Our *exiles* hold stories of adverse experiences. The prevalence of adversity reminds us of the universality of suffering. From complex childhood trauma to routine ruptures in adult relationships, we are all inevitably wounded. Our pain is both exquisitely personal and a means of connecting to the larger community of fellow survivors—survivors of a fallen world.

Of course, there are differing degrees of adversity. In fact, the same event can impact different people differently. The meaning we make of our experiences, our relational context, the history that precedes an event, and even our biology, among other things, combine to shape an event's unique impact upon us. Some challenges are likely to significantly affect most people who experience them. However, some adverse experiences are more subtle and might be quickly dismissed or minimized.

For example, emotional neglect includes a parent persistently denying a child's discomfort. A client once described a scene from her childhood when she first learned to ride a bike. She didn't see a hose stretched across the sidewalk. When she ran over it, she fell, tangled in the bike. Bruised and bleeding, she tearfully called for her mother, who was standing nearby. Her mother ignored her and continued playing with her younger sister.

The seven-year-old girl became an exile in this client's internal family. She carried the negative belief, "I'm unlovable," with related feelings of shame and despair. She could even feel the pain in her body from being tangled in the bike. The emotional intensity of these experiences, and the threat they pose to our well-being, create the most potent memories in our brains.[15]

No one entirely escapes the impact of adversity. We all have exiles in our internal family carrying burdens that, like toxic waste, seep into our system and affect our functioning. Thankfully, humans are resilient. God gave us the capacity to adapt,

---

15. *The Body Keeps the Score*, Bessel J. van der Kolk, pg. 176

to survive even the most egregious harm. Our internal family includes a team of adapters, our protectors.

Protectors: The Guardians of the Internal Family

Just as God's exquisite design provides the resources necessary to thrive, it also includes the capacity to adapt to the inevitable challenges we face. Vulnerability is inherent in the human condition, yet it poses a threat. It's difficult to function if we are overwhelmed by distorted beliefs, painful emotions, and distressing sensations and images. From the perspective of IFS, we adapt through protective strategies adopted by internal family members called *protectors*.

Some of those protective strategies are proactive. Similar to a team of corporate risk managers, they want to identify situations that could expose our vulnerabilities and try to avoid them. For example, one client was considering expanding her business. She was excited about using her creativity to fill a niche in the market. But, whenever she attempted to develop a business plan for the new venture, one of her protectors took over. It identified the potential pitfalls, filling her with anxiety and derailing the process. This protector had a positive intention, as is always the case. It meant well, even if it squelched her creativity and confidence. It did not want her to fail at the new venture; it feared she would be overwhelmed by shame.

The proactive protectors' job is to manage other people's perceptions of us and avoid pain from adverse experiences. We refer to this category of protectors as our internal *managers*. Examples of proactive protective strategies adopted by managers in the inner family include control, perfectionism, overfunctioning, caretaking, and criticism (of ourselves and others).

Perhaps you, like me, have a manager who attempts to control others' perceptions by critiquing your physical appearance, making sure you are on time and on task, and privileging work over play. If this manager slips up and you miss an appointment, or your work product isn't flawless, you could hear from an inner critic, one of the most common members of the protective squad in internal families. It might be challenging to remember that this part of you means well, but she does. She thinks if she criticizes you first, you'll avoid the much more difficult experience of being criticized by someone else.

Sometimes, no matter how hard your managers work, current events trigger past experiences, and pain floods the system. That's when another group of protectors takes over: they are the first responders who will do whatever it takes to distract us or numb the pain. Their strategies include dissociating, substance abuse, and binging on food or entertainment. Because they, like firefighters called to your home to douse the flames, don't care about the consequences of saving you from pain, this team of protectors is called *firefighters.*

Fear drives all of your protectors, whether managers or firefighters. They are aware of your exiles and fear that the pain of their wounds will overwhelm you. They will do whatever it takes to protect you.

Their job does not define their essence, however. It's like a uniform they wear. Outside of painful life experiences, your parts are free to contribute in any manner of ways to the whole person you are. It is adversity that causes members of our internal family to adopt a range of roles that help us adapt and survive.

Is There Hope for Healing?

Because none of us avoid the impact of adversity, rather than the ideal scenario of a leader drawing on a plethora of resources to serve an array of intriguing and talented family members, we all have an internal family system impacted by a fallen world. Adverse experiences burden some internal family members—exiles—with distorted beliefs, painful emotions, distressing images, and uncomfortable sensations. Protective internal family members adopt various strategies to avoid or numb pain—adaptations that help us survive overwhelming challenges—but which can leave collateral damage.

Because of the activity of exiles and protectors, the resources reflecting God's image—resources required for healing—are constrained or, in some cases, blocked altogether.

Is there hope for transformation? Is restoration possible? How can the exiles be welcomed home and the protectors freed from their fear-based strategies? How can the Self lead the internal family in harmony with the Spirit, freely accessing all our God-given resources?

While this may be a new way of understanding ourselves, these are not new questions. The sacred texts recording the relationship between God and God's people are full of stories of exile, anguish, and fear-driven strategies undertaken when trust in God eludes us.

And these sacred stories also reveal healing, restoration, and redemption.

As we journey back to ancient times, I will point out the skills required to connect with the most vulnerable human experiences, and I hope you will learn to witness your own heartache. Engaging your God-given imagination—a potent tool for healing—can enable you to connect with people whose struggles reflect your own. In addition, you will learn how to develop relationships with all of the members of your inner family, restoring leadership to the system.

Imagine being able to draw on all of the resources you possess as a bearer of God's image: bringing curiosity and confidence to your hard-working but fearful protectors, offering compassion and connection to your vulnerable exiles, and loving all of the vital parts of yourself unconditionally.

This is *shalom.* This is harmonious co-existence.

Loving ourselves is the often-overlooked element of the Great Commandment. When we do not love ourselves because exiles' pain and protectors' strategies block our hearts, we are not free to love God and others. The healing journey you undertake is not selfish or self-absorbed. It is essential.

Our healing matters because it is the only way to remove the barriers to loving others. Healing wounds held by members of your internal family opens space for curiosity, courage, and clarity in your interactions with others, restoring those relationships. *Shalom* "flows from all of one's relationships being put right–with God, within oneself, and with others."[16]

Spiritual Practice: Cultivating Inner Awareness

Awareness of inner experience is a foundational practice I will encourage throughout this book. In contexts rife with distractions, cultivating the practice

16. https://www.thenivbible.com/blog/meaning-shalom-bible pg.1, Retrieved on 6/8/21

of attending to our inner experience requires some commitment. Underlying the practice of awareness is the premise that there is value in being with whatever we notice without needing it to change—in other words, practicing grace.

Our culture values *doing* over *being*, so part of this practice is to notice the impulse to act or challenge or avoid, without following through on those impulses. Instead, you will notice them, welcome them as a message from a part of you, and connect with them when the time is right to learn more about their story.

I encourage you to use a journal—perhaps one dedicated to exploring your internal family—to note responses and experiences with the spiritual practices throughout this book. Tracking what we notice helps build awareness and supports our commitment to connecting with internal family members.

Through cultivating awareness of your inner experience and connecting with different members of your internal family, you will come to understand and believe that this "internal family" perspective and the practices based on it are a powerful support to healing.

- What arises for you when you consider attending to your inner experience? Do you feel overwhelmed, excited, intrigued, fearful, or a combination of several emotions?

- What environment helps you shift focus from external to internal information? Quiet? Music? Being outdoors? Moving your body?

- Awareness is just the first step in building relationships with members of your internal family. What do you notice inside when you consider building relationships with parts of yourself? Skepticism? Curiosity? Hope? Concern? Confusion? Allow whatever is there to be present without needing it to change.

- Re-read the story of Rachel, the bleeding woman. Notice your responses. What emotions arise? Is there something in your story that connects you to her? Imagine approaching Jesus in a crowd to ask him to meet your needs. What feelings do you notice?

Chapter Two

Who's Listening to Our Stories?

Genesis 16:4-15; 21:8-19

Hagar's preparations for the feast were interrupted by Sarah's raised voice. "Cast out this slave woman with her son; for the son of this slave woman shall not inherit along with my son Isaac."[1]

Hagar froze. Terror gripped her chest and she could barely breathe. After serving their family, including submitting to Sarah's directive to lie with Abraham, *this* would be her fate? Anger rippled through her body. She wanted to scream, to finally shout all the things she felt about the injustice of being powerless over her life.

Where would they go? Her hopes for Ishmael's future, which seemed secure moments ago, died as despair and grief welled up.

How could this be? This was not the outcome Hagar imagined when she obeyed God's instruction to return to Abraham and Sarah the last time she ran away.

Memories filled her mind, alongside those familiar emotions of shame, fear, and rage. She had no choice about getting pregnant by Abraham. The shame she felt from being used to satisfy Sarah's goal provoked a part of her to say, "Put Sarah in her place. You are with child, and she is barren." It felt much better to see Sarah as pathetic than to feel shame. One day, that part took over, and she dared to look at Sarah contemptuously. She might be enslaved, but at least she could conceive a child!

The fleeting feeling of power was quickly replaced by fear as Sarah turned all of her pain-fuled rage upon her. Hagar knew she needed to leave.

---

1. Genesis 21:10, NRSV

Grabbing a few things, she took off into the wilderness, tears blinding her eyes, desperation over her fate welling up inside. She dropped down by a spring of water, wondering how she and her unborn baby would survive.

Just then, a man appeared out of nowhere. He called her name and asked why she was there. He then said, "Return to your mistress and submit to her."[2] Before she could protest, he added, "I will increase your descendants so much that they will be too numerous to count."[3] He told her she was carrying a son, and that his name would be Ishmael, meaning *God hears.*

At first, Hagar was stunned. Then she felt a strange sense of peace and confidence that this was no ordinary man. Imagine! Hagar, the enslaved foreigner, the matriarch of a large family! For the first time since being sold into slavery, the pregnancy gave her status in a family and hope for the future.

"You are El-roi,"[4] she said, the God who sees me. God heard the cries of her heart and saw her suffering. Because of God's assurances, Hagar was confident she could return and cope with being an enslaved person in Abraham and Sarah's household.

But here she was again, years later, her hopes crushed once more. This time, she was forced to leave. Abraham's eyes barely met hers as he handed her a small supply of bread and water and sent her away.

Before long, she and Ishmael were alone in the wilderness. The sun beat down on them, and his lips cracked. She was afraid their water would run out before she found a spring.

A familiar critical inner voice spoke up, "How could you have been so stupid! Sarah would never allow Ishmael to be a brother to Isaac, sharing in Abraham's affections! You must have been delirious when you thought God promised you a future. Now your son is suffering, and it's all your fault."

---

2. Genesis 16:9, NRSV

3. Genesis 16:10, NIV

4. Genesis 16:13. Hagar is the only person in the Canon to give God a name. *Womanist Midrash,* Wilda C. Gafney, pg. 43. The precise Hebrew meaning of El-roi is uncertain, including "God of seeing," and "God who sees" NRSV Study Bible note pg. 34. NIV Study Bible translates El-roi "The God who sees me."

Tears dripped off her chin onto Ishmael's head as he drooped in her arms. The weight of his limp body frightened her; she tried to get more water out of the jug, but it was empty.

The pain of his misery was excruciating. She couldn't watch him die! She put him under a bush, hoping the scant shade would ease his discomfort. Hagar walked just far enough away that she could hear his weak cries without having to watch. Utterly powerless and alone, she dropped her head into her hands, sobbing.

Without warning, a voice said, "Do not be afraid; God has heard the boy crying...Lift the boy and take him by the hand, for I will make him into a great nation."[5]

Was she dreaming? Remembering the promise God made when she was pregnant?

She opened her eyes and saw a well of water. Hope broke through her despair as she rushed over to fill the jug. She ran to Ishmael and gently poured water into his parched mouth. He stirred and began guzzling the water. After taking a long drink, he held his arms up, and she picked him up, overwhelmed with gratitude.

Our Deepest Need

When Hagar fled into the desert wilderness alone, God met her.[6] God named the son she would bear *Ishmael*, meaning "God hears." "God...recognized and responded to Hagar's plight."[7] In an act of worship, Hagar named God *El-roi*, "God who sees."[8] Years later, when Abraham and Sarah sent Hagar away, God heard her son's cries. God witnessed and responded to Hagar's deep despair.

Hagar's name for God describes a witness who sees more than external circumstances. This witness sees the inner world, the soul's turmoil. Hagar experienced what we most need when we are in distress—the presence of a

---

5. Genesis 21:17-18, NIV

6. Genesis 16:7. The NRSV New Interpreter's Study Bible equates the "angel of the Lord" with God, pg. 34. This is consistent with verse 13: "So she named the Lord who spoke to her..."

7. NRSV New Interpreter's Study Bible, pg. 34

8. Genesis 16:13 NIV

compassionate witness. This listener meets our need for connection, comfort, and reassurance.

Hagar was an unlikely candidate for the honor of an intimate connection with God. An enslaved Egyptian whose name meant "foreigner,"[9] she did not have power or status in the household. Powerlessness was a core theme in Hagar's life. She was (presumably) sold by her family into slavery, given to Abraham, then cast off when her son was perceived as a threat.

As modern-day Jesus-followers, familiar with the proclamation of a Kingdom for the outcasts and marginalized, it's difficult to fully appreciate how unexpected God's care for Hagar, an enslaved foreign woman, was. God's provision of care for someone an ancient culture didn't value is a poignant reminder that God's character does not change.

Yet, the lens through which we see God shifts with our circumstances. When intense emotions flood our internal system we lose perspective, disconnecting us from our source of comfort. To restore equilibrium, we need to feel seen, safe, soothed, and secure.[10]

Neuroscientists refer to this as "feeling felt."[11] In his book *The Developing Mind*, Daniel Siegel describes "feeling felt" as an "intense and intimate form of connection...manifested both in words and in nonverbal aspects of communication: facial expressions, eye contact, tone of voice, bodily movement, and timing of responses."[12]

See if you can imagine Hagar "feeling felt" by God. She "put the boy under one of the bushes" and "went off and sat down about a bowshot away, for she thought, 'I cannot watch the boy die.'"[13] The shame of being unable to save her son and the despair over his suffering must have been overwhelming. At the most excruciating moment, she heard, "Do not be afraid. God has heard the boy crying

---

9. *Womanist Midrash*, Wilda C. Gafney, pg. 34

10. *Parenting from the Inside Out*, Daniel J. Siegel & Mary Hartzell, pg. 108

11. *The Developing Mind*, Daniel J. Siegel, pg. 117

12. Ibid, pg. 117

13. Genesis 21:15-16 NIV

as he lies there."[14] The compassionate and reassuring voice would have flooded Hagar with relief. God resolved her terrible dilemma by lovingly guiding her to water, restoring their lives and the promise of their future.

When we're overwhelmed we need an attuned listener. Unconditional acceptance of our emotional state creates the safety for vulnerable, intimate connection. We feel seen and understood. As Siegel says, "We have a sense that we are not alone in this world because our self is connected to something larger than the boundaries of our own skin."[15]

An Ever-Present Witness

On the night of the Last Supper, Jesus prepared the disciples for unimaginable trauma and the loss of his physical presence by reassuring them that he would not abandon them. "I will not leave you as orphans; I will come to you."[16] "I will ask the Father, and he will give you another advocate to help you and be with you forever...You know him because he lives with you and will be in you."[17]

The intimate connection Jesus' followers enjoyed during his earthly ministry would not be lost. The Spirit "helps us in our weakness."[18] Whatever our specific challenge, our fundamental need is a connection with a loving presence, an attuned listener, and a guide. Jesus taught his followers that the Spirit would be his "ongoing presence," their "teacher and witness."[19]

Jesus reassured his followers that they would have "the Spirit of truth."[20] What could be more true than the need for loving relationships? God "is love,"[21]

---

14. Genesis 21:17 NIV

15. *Parenting from the Inside Out*, Daniel J. Siegel & Mary Hartzell, pg. 85

16. John 14:18, NIV

17. John 14:16-17, NIV

18. Romans 8:26, NIV

19. NRSV The New Interpreter's Study Bible, pg. 1941

20. John 14:17, 16:13, NIV

21. 1 John 4:8, NIV

expressed as a community of loving persons. This is a community where we can "feel felt" when we are in distress, where we are continually "connected to something larger than the boundaries of our own skin."[22]

Each manifestation of the Triune God reveals God's desire to be in a loving relationship with us, which supports our needs. Hagar met this same God who sees and hears our needs. Jesus' healing ministry reoriented people to the heart of God's purpose—to restore *shalom.* The Spirit carries on that ministry working in and through the community of God's people. Theologian William C. Placher writes, "If we Christians understand the doctrine of the Trinity aright, we will realize that it implies that God is not about power and self-sufficiency and the assertion of authority but about mutuality and equality and love."[23]

We are created in the image of this Triune God.

Another Witness

The image of God in us (the Self) is an inherent aspect of God's provision, part of meeting our need for loving relationships; it is our inner witness. We have a listener who joins the Spirit in tending to our distress.

As I explained briefly in chapter one, as Dr. Schwartz encouraged clients to share their inner experiences, one of the most surprising discoveries was the universal presence of healing qualities. "Client after client, the same mindfully curious, calm, confident, and often even compassionate part would pop up out of the blue, *and that part seemed to know how to relate internally in a healing way.*"[24] Dr. Schwartz writes, "After thousands of hours doing this work, I can say with certainty that Self is in everybody."[25]

All of humanity bears God's image. God endowed us with a leader of our inner family for daily living, who also possesses qualities profoundly useful for serving the needs of the entire internal system. While there is no limit to the ways we reflect

---

22. *Parenting from the Inside Out*, Daniel J. Siegel & Mary Hartzell, pg. 85

23. *Narratives of a Vulnerable God: Christ, Theology, and Scripture*, William C. Placher, pg. 55

24. *No Bad Parts: Healing Trauma & Restoring Wholeness with The Internal Family Systems Model*, Richard C. Schwartz, P.hD., pg. 22. Italics mine.

25. Ibid, pg. 22

God's image—no limit to the myriad facets of love—the eight C characteristics are highly relevant for healing. These qualities of the Self, once again, are curiosity, connection, compassion, calm, confidence, creativity, courage, and clarity.

Think of a challenge you're currently facing. Perhaps there's a complicated relationship you're navigating, or you feel overwhelmed or anxious by your circumstances. Which of these C qualities would be helpful? For example, courage and confidence help us establish and maintain healthy boundaries in relationships. Calm and connection soothe anxious inner family members. Compassion welcomes parts just as they are, validating their feelings.

It might be surprising to learn that, as essential as all C qualities are for healing, *curiosity* is the foundation of the relationship between the Self and other internal family members.

When the blind man cried out to Jesus, Jesus asked, "What do you want me to do for you?"[26] Jesus knew the man was blind; he heard his cries for mercy. Why would Jesus ask him what he needed instead of simply healing him? Jesus was genuinely curious; he wasn't manipulative. His question provided a sacred space for the man to express his needs and stand in his own agency.

God met Hagar in the wilderness the first time she left, asking, "Where have you come from, and where are you going?"[27] Later, when she was sent back into the wilderness by Abraham and Sarah, God asked, "What is the matter, Hagar?"[28] Surely, God already knows these answers, but by offering genuine curiosity, connection is facilitiated. It sends a message that it is safe to share our needs, whatever they may be.

When Self meets a member of the internal family with curiosity, they almost always (in my experience) feel calm. Self contains the wisdom conferred by God that resources are available for healing. This calm confidence is contagious. Parts of the inner system realize they are no longer alone—one of their greatest fears. They relax, and the connection with the Self deepens.

Members of the internal family hold a variety of emotions, beliefs, sensations, and images from their experiences. Imagine all that they hold as a barrier

---

26. Mark 10:51, NIV

27. Genesis 16:8, NIV

28. Genesis 21:17, NIV

blocking their perspective. Self provides clarity, helping them see solutions to their dilemmas.

Often, courage and creativity fuel the healing journey. Courage enables us to turn toward the most painful stories without flinching. Creativity, the power of our imagination, facilitates relationships with inner family members, bringing them to life.

As relationships between Self and parts develop, compassion flows. The reflection of God's image, the Self leads in harmony with the Holy Spirit. Self sees with the eyes of the Spirit, extending unconditional love and gracious acceptance to each internal family member.

Curiosity and connection.

Calm and confidence.

Clarity, courage, and creativity.

Compassion.

These qualities, facets of the image of God in us, are inate, evident from birth.

When my first grandchild was about five months old, my daughter sent a video of her reaching for their dog's ear. (Thankfully, this dog is open to all forms of affection!) She was *curious* and *confident* as she grabbed the ear and tried to put it in her mouth. A few months later, she blew kisses to her daddy in another favorite video, reflecting *connection*. Imagine the *courage* required to pull up and stand—or take steps—for the first time!

Additional Healing Resources

Let's look at a few more healing resources you possess—the Ps. Over time, Dr. Schwartz also recognized the existence and healing power of several P qualities: presence, patience, perspective, persistence, and playfulness.[29]

Can you think of someone whose presence radiates love? That is the *presence* of the Self. There's a connection and flow of energy between the Self and God, and between the Self and all internal family members. The presence of the Self creates a sacred space of connection and hope.

---

29. *No Bad Parts: Healing Trauma & Restoring Wholeness with The Internal Family Systems Model*, Richard C. Schwartz, PhD, pg. 125

Self is inherently *patient*. Our most vulnerable experiences are hidden deep in our inner world. Layers of protection surround them to keep their pain from overwhelming the system. Your internal family members have played roles and carried burdens for many years. They often experienced powerlessness, a lack of control over their circumstances. Developing a relationship at the pace *they* choose restores their sense of agency. It is respectful and builds trust in the Self as a resource for healing. Members of the inner family sometimes attempt to rush the process; they are desperate for healing. The truest stories, however, often unfold over many hours and many encounters. The gentle patience of the Self helps protective parts to gain trust and vulnerable parts to emerge.

Leading in harmony with the Spirit, the Self patiently fosters connection with different inner family members and *persistently* seeks healing—aligned with the same goal as the Spirit, our divine Counselor. The protective members of the internal family, whom I introduced briefly, work to avoid and distract us from pain. Persistently reminding them that Self and Spirit can handle whatever arises keeps the healing journey on track.

When Hagar left her son, sobbing as she waited for him to die, she could not see beyond her immediate crisis. Adversity narrows our understanding of what is possible because our prefrontal cortex (our thinking brain) goes offline during times of overwhelm. The parts of us who experience adversity are locked into scenes—stuck in the time events occurred. Their protectors—members of the internal family who adapted to circumstances by adopting various roles—have blinders that block their ability to see a broader picture. Healing requires the resource of *perspective*. Self, drawing on God-given resources, can see the entire inner landscape. In an external example of what Self and Spirit provide internally, God gently offered a broader perspective to Hagar, showing her a well with life-giving water.[30]

The final P quality might be unexpected. How does *playfulness* support healing? A neuroscientist who studied emotions discovered our brains have seven

30. Genesis 21:19

primary affective circuits, including *play*.[31] Why would play be as crucial for survival as nurturing our young, fearing threats, and seeking connection with others?

Research shows play, or "social joy," is essential for social bonding,[32] and the bonds we form through play contribute to the safety required for healing. The playful moments I experience with clients, all of whom are doing the courageous work of healing from trauma and adversity, strengthen our therapeutic relationship. Play reminds the burdened members of the internal family of what they lost and what healing restores. Joyful energy spontaneously emerges, providing hope, which further sustains the process.

Resources Can Be Constrained

We are born with the capacity to connect, which is essential for survival. Our brains and nervous systems contain the infrastructure necessary to support loving relationships. As I said before, the qualities reflecting God's image and the resources available to Self are intact from birth, they are not developmental outcomes. While they manifest differently over our lifespan, they are God-given qualities present in everyone. Congruent with God's design, Dr. Schwartz discovered, "Self cannot be damaged, the Self doesn't have to develop, and the Self possesses its own wisdom about how to heal internal as well as external relationships."[33]

While it's true that nothing can damage these resources, they can be blocked or constrained. Remember, the Self is not the only member of the internal family! Even with the presence and power of the Holy Spirit in us, the activity of other parts of the system restricts access to our healing resources.

---

31. Davis, K.L. & Montag, C. (2019). Selected Principles of Pankseppian Affective Neuroscience. Frontiers in Neuroscience, volume 12, pg 1. https://www.researchgate.net/publication/330447907_Selected_Principles_of_Pankseppian_Affective_Neuroscience, retrieved 3/10/22

32. Ibid, pg. 2

33. *No Bad Parts: Healing Trauma & Restoring Wholeness with The Internal Family Systems Model*, Richard C. Schwartz, P.hD., pg. 22-23

Reread Hagar's story above. Can you see how distress blocked access to her God-given confidence and courage?

The activity of her internal family members, some burdened by pain and despair, others reacting with anger and criticism, blocked Hagar's Self. She didn't have access to confidence or courage. She—however understandably—lost sight of God's promise, the perspective and clarity she needed to navigate challenges with Sarah. She didn't feel compassion that would enable her to understand and connect with Sarah's pain. Self was there, but other members of the inner family blocked it. I also imagine a critical member of her internal family would berate her for ending up in this predicament. She was powerless to help her son and desperately alone.

This is why developing relationships with your internal family members is essential. As you restore the Self-leadership of your internal family, you will have more access to qualities supporting healing and more capacity to listen to the Spirit.

Spiritual Practice: Cultivating Awareness of the Self

These practices support your awareness of the God-given resources available when the Self leads your internal family. The more Self-led we are, the more space we have in our internal system to discern the voice and movements of the Spirit. The goal is not to lead independently of the Spirit but to lead in harmony with the Spirit. In truth, the Self does not actually contradict the Spirit. The more Self-led you are, the more attentive and responsive you will be to the movement of the Spirit. You are practicing awareness and *unblending*—differentiating Self from other inner family members.

In your journal, write down the 8 Cs: curiosity, calm, connection, compassion, clarity, confidence, courage, and creativity. You can simply write the words, or if you are a more visual or kinetic processor, you can use markers, crayons, or colored pencils and depict them creatively, or use objects to represent them.

- Spend time focusing on each quality.
    - It can be helpful to look up definitions in a dictionary or think of examples of times you drew on a particular resource.
    - Notice how your body feels when you focus on each resource. Do they have different energy? Calm probably feels different than compassion or curiosity.
- Which resources feel the most compelling to you?
- Do any of the resources feel desirable but unattainable?
- Note responses and reflections in your journal.

Bring a current challenge to mind. What do you feel when you look at the list of resources you possess, the gifts God gave you for healing?

- Does the reality that you possess healing resources bring a sense of calm and confidence?
- Do you feel hopeful about healing?
- Does part of you feel hopeful, but another part is doubtful or despairing? Parts are often polarized—at odds with one another.
    - Shift attention to the part of you that is not optimistic. Just be with them without needing them to change. Their hesitation is valid; it reflects their experiences. Notice if there is more calm in your system as you offer your presence to them. Your presence conveys grace—loving acceptance of them just as they are.
- It is helpful to use your journal to keep track of parts you identify. You might want to return to them in later exercises.

CHAPTER THREE

THE CHARACTERS IN OUR STORIES

1 & 2 SAMUEL & SELECT PSALMS

A Complex Man: Act One

David felt like one of the lions who preyed on his sheep. Every muscle tensed for action, energy surging through his body, his mind sharp. As Goliath approached, he drew strength from the assurance of God's provision. He was certain he could do what others said could not be done.

Visions of glory, of the reward Saul was offering, captivated him.[1] David imagined slaying Goliath, and the life he would enjoy as a result. He felt the thrill of anticipation. No more tending sheep or being the errand boy to his older brothers. He would have wealth and the king's favor!

With every step forward, David felt more disgusted with the Israelite soldiers who feared Goliath so much. He was just a youth, and he wasn't afraid of Goliath, the loudmouth bully taunting the troops. How could they be so easily cowed? The living God would deliver this enemy to him, he was convinced of it.

David thought back on his childhood anointing, surely it was for this moment. Energized by clarity and courage, David declared, "I come against you in the name of the Lord Almighty, the God of the armies of Israel, whom you have defied."[2]

The victory was even sweeter than he had imagined. Entering Jerusalem and seeing people singing and dancing in the streets celebrating, David felt a rush of

---

1. 1 Samuel 17:25, NIV

2. 1 Samuel 17:45, NIV

pride.[3] Confident in his skill and mission, he was eager to serve the king to defeat the enemies of the living God. All of Israel would know his name.

A Complex Man: Act Two

David felt so connected to Saul when he played for him, their souls soaring together as they rode the current of the music. He imagined he was a conduit for God's love as he watched Saul shift from frenetic pacing to contemplative silence.

It was confusing when dark moods would overwhelm Saul, and he tried to attack David. But he was the king, surely he carried burdens difficult to imagine. David played on, though his confidence was shaken. All seemed to be well, as his faithfulness was rewarded with command of a thousand men![4]

It was gratifying to represent Saul on the battlefield. With each successful mission, David's confidence in the Lord's presence and guidance grew.[5]

Then he learned that Saul had sent men to kill him![6] Terrified, he fled, but he could not understand how the king could be this angry with him. Fear and confusion muddled his mind and exhausted his body.

The constant need to evade Saul began to take a toll. In moments of terror or despair, David cried out to God. "Have mercy on me, Lord, for I am faint; heal me, Lord, for my bones are in agony. My soul is in deep anguish. How long, Lord, how long? Turn, Lord, and deliver me; save me because of your unfailing love."[7]

David felt God's protection when he and his men narrowly escaped Saul and fled to the desert.[8] The cool air in the cave offered a welcome respite from the desert heat—and from the relentless anxiety of being pursued. David felt weary, discouraged, and frustrated by having to focus on evading Saul instead of fighting the enemies of the Lord. He prayed, "Will you forget me forever, Lord? How long

3. 1 Samuel 18:6-7, NIV

4. 1 Samuel 18:13, NIV

5. 1 Samuel 18:14, NIV

6. 1 Samuel 19:11, NIV

7. Psalm 6:2-4, NIV

8. 1 Samuel 23:26-28, NIV

will you hide your face from me? How long must I wrestle with my thoughts and day after day have sorrow in my heart? How long will my enemy triumph over me?"[9]

Mired in despair, David was startled when one of his men rushed over, saying, "Saul's at the front of the cave! Now's your chance to get rid of him!" Could this be the answer to his prayers? The surge of adrenaline made his heart pound as he crept toward Saul.

David could hear echoes of his men's voices saying the Lord had given him this opportunity to deal with his enemy.[10] An inner voice said, "Saul deserves this!" and David drew his knife from its sheath. But he froze, as memories of their good years together floated through his mind. Gripped by indecision, another inner voice said, "Just show him you're not a threat." David reached forward and cut off a corner of Saul's cloak, then retreated to the back of the cave.

Guilt washed over him; his face felt hot, and his body was slick with sweat. Remorse gripped his gut over how close he'd come to harming the Lord's anointed king. He ran out of the cave, calling after Saul.

Regret bumped up against anger over Saul's relentless efforts to kill him. He told Saul, "I have not wronged you, but you are hunting me down to take my life. May the Lord judge between you and me. And may the Lord avenge the wrongs you have done to me, but my hand will not touch you."[11]

David kept his vow. He felt confident the Lord would protect him. Saul was in God's hands.[12]

Having resolved to trust the Lord with Saul, David wrote, "The Lord is my shepherd, I shall not want. He makes me lie down in green pastures; he leads me beside still waters; he restores my soul. He leads me in right paths for his name's sake. Even though I walk through the darkest valley, I fear no evil; for you are with me; your rod and your staff—they comfort me."[13]

---

9. Psalm 13:1-2, NIV

10. 1 Samuel 24:4, NIV

11. 1 Samuel 24:11-12, NIV

12. 1 Samuel 26:9-10, NIV

13. Psalm 23:1-4, NRSV

A Complex Man: Act Three

King David enjoyed victorious battles wherever he went.[14] One year, he decided to remain in Jerusalem while his army to war.[15] It felt strange to be in the city, knowing his soldiers were subduing the enemies of God without his leadership. David felt a rush of adrenaline as he relived his many victories. He never questioned his purpose when fighting one of Israel's foes.

It was too quiet in his room in the palace. He liked being in a tent among his men, connected to them and God, who faithfully guided and protected him from harm. Bored and restless, David went for a walk on the roof.

Tonight the view of his city, a sight that would usually fill him with gratitude for God's blessings, left him agitated by a nagging sense of purposelessness. What was he going to do while his men were on the battlefield?

Then he saw her. Bathing upon her rooftop, she was oblivious to his gaze.

He was captivated by her beauty. His body tingled, and his heart raced. All thoughts of battle were replaced by one thought: I must have her.

David called for his servant. He pointed her out and told him to go find out about her. While he waited for the servant to return, he felt a familiar rush of anticipation, the energy that prepared him for battle. This woman was a prize worth fighting for!

The servant rushed in, saying, "She is Bathsheba, the daughter of Eliam and the wife of Uriah the Hittite."[16]

Good. The men in her family are away. I can send for her, he thought. Sending a group would convey the message that this was not a request but a command from her king, so he sent several men to her.

When she arrived, David felt the thrill of victory coursing through his body. Taking her to his bed felt like a triumph in battle.

Her pregnancy was an unfortunate complication, but David quickly developed a plan. Send for Uriah. With a wife as beautiful as Bathsheba, he should be eager

---

14. 2 Samuel 8:6,14, NIV

15. 2 Samuel 11:1, NIV

16. 2 Samuel 11:3, NIV

to have sex with her, protecting David from the penalty of sleeping with another man's wife—death.[17]

But Uriah did what David would not. He insisted on avoiding his wife while his men were still on the battlefield. David clenched his teeth, rage rising in his guts. Desperate to get Uriah into bed with Bathsheba, David plied him with alcohol. Maybe if he were drunk, he would want to lie with her as he should.

It felt like he was going to explode. How could this man be so high-and-mighty!? How dare he thwart the king! A new plan took hold; David felt a steely calm. He sent Uriah back to the front lines where the fighting was fiercest, asking Joab to ensure Uriah would not survive the battle.

David felt a pang of remorse, but another part of him pushed it aside, saying, "There's no time for that! You need to protect your legacy. Now that Uriah is dead, Bathsheba can become your wife." Relief washed away his nagging concerns as David saw he'd regained control; the circumstances of their son's conception would remain secret.

Days later, David welcomed Nathan, hoping for another blessing from the Lord. Hearing Nathan's strange story about a rich man with herds of sheep and cattle stealing a lamb from a poor man filled him with rage. How could someone have such a callous disregard for another person's cherished blessings?[18]

When Nathan said, "You are the man," David felt clammy and nauseous. His knees buckled and he could barely stand. Nathan's words pierced his soul. Hearing the litany of the Lord's gifts, followed by Nathan's indictment, filled David with shame. He knew he had violated God's laws; his actions *were* evil.[19]

As David's thoughts raced, imagining how he could restore his relationship with God, Nathan delivered the final blow. His utter contempt for the Lord would cost his infant son his life.[20]

---

17. Deuteronomy 22:22, NIV

18. 2 Samuel 12:1-6, NIV

19. 2 Samuel 12:7-13, NIV

20. 2 Samuel 12:14, NIV

A Portrait of Multiplicity

How do we make sense of a character as complex as David? He's introduced as the God's anointed, powerfully filled with the Spirit of the Lord.[21] How appropriate for him to believe he could prevail over Goliath, who had been taunting the Israelites for weeks! Yet, there are indications of David's complexity in this familiar story. He's captivated by the prize the king will pay to the man who kills Goliath, asking three times to confirm it. It strains credulity to take at face value David's account of taking a sheep from the mouth of a bear or lion—or grabbing a wild animal by the hair so he could kill it—to convince Saul of his capability. Could he have been so convinced of his skill that he was willing to exaggerate?

And still, when David could justifiably protect himself by killing Saul, he is overcome by guilt for even entertaining the thought. Yet, unfortunately, in relationships with women, his conscience is blocked by a combination of forces we'll examine.

For some, David is held up as a clear hero, often lauded as a man after God's own heart. But he's a complex person with a complicated story. Pay attention to how you felt as we unpacked some of those complexities. Do you want to turn away from this story, or do you see David's conflicting impulses in your own story? A nuanced portrait of David reveals multiplicity—an inner family with a leader and members who play various roles, some of which block his best qualities.

When Self Leads the Inner Family

The qualities revealed in David's finest moments emerge when Self—the leader of the inner family bearing God's image—leads. The survey of David's victories—military and moral—reflects the heart God saw in David. While people "look at the outward appearance," David was chosen because "the Lord looks at the heart."[22]

Qualities of Self permeate many chapters in David's story. His confidence and commitment to God were evident when he offered to fight Goliath. He humbly

---

21. 1 Samuel 16:13, NIV

22. 1 Samuel 16:7, NIV

sought the Lord's guidance before making decisions, reflecting the ideal of Self leading in harmony with God.[23] During the years when Saul pursued him, David's connection with God sustained him. This is not leadership independent of God; this is leadership grounded in God's strength and mercy.

In one of the greatest tests of his character, David chose not to harm Saul. Despite men suggesting God was giving Saul to David "to deal with as you wish,"[24] David regretted even taking a piece of Saul's cloak. His integrity and courage drove him to confront Saul to protest his innocence while swearing he would not harm anyone in Saul's family.[25] David kept his promise the second time he had an opportunity to kill Saul.[26]

Integrity was one of his most outstanding qualities. When he chose not to murder Saul, he lived up to what God saw in his heart. He reflected God's mercy. David was also able to forgive Saul; he sincerely lamented his death.[27]

David's virtue impacted Saul. The first time David spared his life, Saul wept, saying, "You are more righteous than I...You have treated me well, but I have treated you badly".[28] The second time, Saul confessed, saying, "I have sinned...Surely I have acted like a fool and have been terribly wrong".[29] Self-leadership can spur others to repentance because they see the contrast between their behavior and behavior motivated by love.

Self is steadfast, an anchor for the inner system during storms. David felt the full array of emotions during tumultuous years of battles and evading Saul. However, his psalms reveal a heart committed to faithfulness; his abiding, intimate relationship with God is evident everywhere. He trusts God when circumstances are dire, terrifying, and overwhelming, and he praises God for blessings.

---

23. For example, see 1 Samuel 23:1-2

24. 1 Samuel 24:4, NIV

25. 1 Samuel 24:21-22, NIV

26. 1 Samuel 26:23, NIV

27. 2 Samuel 1:19-27, NIV

28. 1 Samuel 24:17, NIV

29. 1 Samuel 26:21, NIV

David's Self is also evident in his relationships with others. Self is compelling. Loving energy—expressed as courage, clarity, and confidence—drew many people to David. Soldiers followed him into battle, people celebrated his victories, and Jonathan treated him like a beloved brother.

Nathan's prophecy, the promise that "your house and your kingdom will endure forever," elicited humility, not vanity, further evidence of Self-leadership. "Who am I, Sovereign Lord, and what is my family that you have brought me this far?"[30] In David's lengthy prayer, he gives God the glory. "How great you are, Sovereign Lord! There is no one like you, and there is no God but you..."[31]

Internal Family Members Sometimes Take The Lead

David's shining moments are like our own. When the Self leads our inner family, we draw on God-given resources like courage, compassion, and clarity to live out our purpose or navigate challenges. We maintain perspective when threats loom. Relationships are satisfying, and we feel connected to God. Integrity and mercy guide our choices; we receive life's blessings with humility and gratitude.

Wouldn't it be a lovely world if Self always led the internal family?

Yet, we, like God—whose image we bear—are multiple. Ideally, our inner family members contribute important qualities, talents, and abilities. Our unique combination of internal family members is a rich reflection of God's creativity. When all members work in harmony under the leadership of Self and Spirit, relationships—with ourselves, God, and others—are loving and mutually satisfying. We experience *shalom.*

Our various inner family members also help us adapt to adversity, reflecting God's creative design. This is necessary to survive. However, challenges can prompt inner family members to adopt roles that block or constrain the Self. Generally, parts that usurp leadership from the Self are trying to protect us from a threat or are attempting to meet our needs. All parts of us are well-intentioned, but they are sometimes motivated to act out of fear or pain. When that occurs, our thoughts, emotions, and behaviors—the activity of our parts— can be perplexing or even destructive.

---

30. 2 Samuel 7:18, NIV

31. 2 Samuel 7:22, NIV

One of the ways our inner family members adapt is by internalizing values and norms from the surrounding culture, including family, ethnicity, nationality, gender, race, socioeconomic status, etc. Some of these cultural norms conflict with our values. However, operating outside cultural norms can make us feel like outsiders. Being an outsider is one of the greatest threats to survival, so parts of us usurp leadership of the system—bypassing our values and principles—in order to comply with the culture, to go along to get along.

Cultural norms—and how internal family members adapt to them—provide insight into David's relationship with his first wife, Michal. This episode in David's story reveals the impact on others when our parts take over leadership from Self.

Michal, Saul's daughter, was in love with David.[32] Michal risked her father's wrath to help David escape the men Saul sent to kill him,[33] but the text is silent about David's feelings for Michal. He doesn't express gratitude for her help or reciprocate her love. Nor does he protest when Saul gives her to another man.[34]

However, when having Michal as his wife could secure the loyalty of northern Israelites aligned with Saul, David wants her back.[35] She had been married to her new husband for years, and when she was taken away from him, he "went with her, weeping behind her all the way."[36] This time, Michal's feelings aren't noted, but we know her husband loved her, perhaps in a way David never had. Yet, as part of a deal negotiated by powerful men, Michal was torn from that marriage and returned to David like property.

David's callous treatment of Michal, led by parts of him who absorbed cultural norms about women as property and his right to use her as a pawn, blocked his heart and constrained those parts of him that were sensitive to injustice. One of the highlights of David's story, the procession with the ark into Jerusalem, is celebrated as an example of joyful, unrestrained worship. However, Michal's response shows the impact of David's mistreatment of her. The text says that she watched David from a window, "and when she saw [him] leaping and dancing before the Lord,

32. 1 Samuel 18:20, NIV

33. 1 Samuel 19:11-17, NIV

34. 1 Samuel 25:44, NIV

35. This motivation is suggested in notes in both NIV and NRSV Study Bibles.

36. 2 Samuel 3:16, NIV

she despised him in her heart."[37] She confronted David, mocking him for "going around half-naked in full view of the slave girls of his servants as any vulgar fellow would."[38] David defended himself, insensitive to Michal's pain.

This sad chapter in David's story reveals his repugnant—yet culturally congruent—attitude toward a wife who loved him and was punished for supporting him.[39] Michal's reactions reflect the impact of David's disregard and disrespect. Having felt the impact of inner family members who blocked David's heart, she sees him through the eyes of her own parts who, in turn, block her heart also.

Michal's story illustrates how internal family members respond when people are not Self-led. David's Self did not lead during interactions with Michal. There's no evidence he cared for her or was aware of the impact of his behavior on her. David treated her like property. While that was the cultural norm, it was never God's intention for human relationships. As a result, Michal's pain provoked parts of her to react with understandable disgust.

Disinterest and selfishness blocked David's heart. In response, Michal's love turned to loathing and, I imagine, grief. The last thing we learn about Michal is that she "had no children to the day of her death."[40] Her fate was to be a "living widow."[41] That David could be so persistently callous to Michal indicates these were prominent parts of his inner system. They reemerge when David encounters Bathsheba.

---

37. 2 Samuel 6:16, NIV

38. 2 Samuel 6:20, NIV

39. While the text is not explicit about Saul's reason for giving Michal to a new husband, it's reasonable, given Saul's character, to assume it was vindictive.

40. 2 Samuel 6:23, NIV

41. This term is from 2 Samuel 20:3, noted by Wil Gafney in *Womanist Midrash*, pg. 196

How Could This Happen?

Understanding how inner family members can take over from Self helps explain how a leader celebrated as a "man after God's own heart"[42] could sin so grievously.

We don't know why David remained in Jerusalem while his army went into battle. His triumph over Goliath, the first of many military victories, earned loyalty from his troops and adoration from the people, culminating in his being named king of Israel. Adrenaline-filled years of evading Saul and battling enemies were David's norm, which surely impacted the roles played by his internal family members. Constant exposure to risk results in hypervigilance; parts of David would have been like sentries, always on duty and ready to fight.

Action-oriented members of the internal family do not like boredom. They seek the rush of a challenge. On that sleepless night when David first saw Bathsheba, she represented the conquest these parts of David sought.

From his interactions with Michal, we are already familiar with culturally indoctrinated parts of David that viewed women as property and prioritized his needs over theirs.

It's also conceivable that part of David's system felt worthless if he wasn't on the battlefield. Shame, one of our most painful emotions, accompanies worthlessness. This kind of burden poses a significant internal threat, prompting parts of our system to react to deal with it.

When David saw Bathsheba bathing, the emotions and sensations in his body were so consuming they blocked Self.

This happens to all of us at times. Think of a time when you were filled with rage, lust, or longing. Did you act impulsively? What were the consequences?

Our emotions provide information and energy for action. There's nothing wrong with any of them or with the intention of parts holding them. However, they are not equipped to lead the system.

There was nothing inherently wrong with parts of David who might have longed for the adrenaline rush of battle or reacted to the shame of feeling worthless. But they needed a leader to evaluate the emotions and impulses they carried so that he could act with clarity and consideration for others. When the parts of us

42. Acts 13:22, NIV

holding intense emotions take over, we often do things we later regret. Recall Paul's lament: "I do not understand what I do. For what I want to do I do not do, but what I hate I do."[43]

Acting independently of Self, the parts who longed for conquest, parts who saw women as property, and those reacting to the threat of shame led David to his most hateful act—raping Bathsheba.

Interestingly, biblical commentaries on this passage reveal ambivalence about charging David, a hero of the Bible, with something as serious as sexual assault. The NIV Study Bible note says, "Bathsheba appears to have had little choice in this adulterous relationship with David because of his disproportionately greater power and authority."[44]

Little choice? "Adulterous relationship"—as though Bathsheba participated willingly?

The NRSV Study Bible note is more explicit about her lack of choice but says, "Having learned that the men of Bathsheba's family are away and that she, therefore, is defenseless, David sends people to bring her to him. She is not consulted; thus, this episode is similar to rape."[45]

Similar to rape?

The reluctance to refer to David's encounter with Bathsheba as rape might reflect our difficulty in accepting David's complex character.

Theologian Wil Gafney highlights both the cultural and religious contexts when she writes, "The absolute power of an ancient Near Eastern monarch combined with the absence of her husband's protection greatly reduces Bathsheba's ability to consent to the sexual encounter...To come when beckoned by the king does not imply consent."[46] Gafney asserts, "Nathan and God treat David as a rapist by condemning him [and] not imputing sin to Bathsheba as

---

43. Romans 7:15, NIV

44. NIV Study Bible, Zondervan 2020, pg. 497

45. The New Interpreter's Study Bible (NRSV), Abingdon Press 2003, pg. 455

46. *Womanist Midrash*, Wil Gafney, pg. 214

a complicit, consenting person. Their treatment of her is consistent with the treatment of women who are raped in the Torah statutes."[47]

Members of David's internal family usurped the leadership of his personhood, with devastating results. As often happens when we act impulsively—when the Self does not lead—one wrong choice leads to a cascade of bad decisions.

Bathsheba's unintended pregnancy—the penalty for which would be death for both of them—provoked parts of David to concoct the plans involving Uriah. Imagine the part who crafted the plan, another who desperately reacted when it didn't work, and yet another who could so thoroughly block David's heart that he could send Uriah—one of David's own mighty soldiers, and a man David correctly discerns as righteous—to his death.

David's lust for power, excitement, and conquest blocked his highest and best Self. He satisfied his needs at Bathsheba's expense and killed a husband for whom she grieved—more evidence she did not consent to the encounter.[48] The death penalty for his crime fell on Uriah, a man of honor.

What a tragic episode.

When David was Self-led, he routinely consulted the Lord before making plans. His psalms display a practice of turning to God with all of his heart, soul, mind, and strength. Yet, he had internal family members who could so thoroughly block his heart that he abused women, and ordered the murder of a righteous man.

When we are Self-led, multiplicity enhances our functioning. We bring a unique blend of characteristics to our work and relationships. Our inner family members also internalize and adapt to life experiences. They adopt various roles to help us navigate challenges or meet essential needs. This reflects God's creative design.

However, parts take over leadership from the Self when our inner system reacts to a threat—to some kind of pain. They block or constrain our God-given resources, and their strategies—despite being well-intentioned—can be dysfunctional and destructive.

David's story shows how we can be both people who share God's heart—who have a Self capable of unconditional love in all its forms—and can hurt others. Pain provokes our extreme parts. Whether you resonate with David's lowest points,

---

47. Ibid, pg. 215

48. 2 Samuel 11:26, NIV

with the people harmed by him, or both, understanding how pain influences our internal families is the next step on the journey to shalom.

Spiritual Practice: Embracing Multiplicity

As you experience the practices for this chapter, I encourage you to use your journal to record insights, reflections, questions, and the parts you identify.

- Turn your attention inside and notice your response to the concept that you are "multiple." Remember, the goal of awareness is to be present with whatever arises without needing it to change. For example, if you notice skepticism or confusion, accept it as a natural aspect of learning something new. If you have conflicting thoughts or emotions, consider the possibility that this reflects different members of your internal family.

- Reflect on the Apostle Paul's lament: "I do not understand my own actions. For I do not do what I want, but I do the very thing I hate" (Romans 7:15, NRSV). Can you relate to Paul? How do you feel if I suggest that behavior you "hate" does not define your whole identity?

- In IFS therapy, a guiding principle is that all parts are welcome. To welcome parts of us whose activity is disruptive or problematic, we must remember that parts have positive intentions—a desire to help somehow—no matter their strategy or the outcome. And, their strategy or job is not their true essence. It is something they do to serve the internal family. (Later in the book, we will cover how we can help them give up jobs that are no longer needed.)

    - What quality or behavior do you wish you didn't have?

    - How does your perspective shift when you think of it as a way to avoid or suppress pain?

- For example, imagine if you are frequently angry but later feel remorse for outbursts. Rather than identifying yourself as "an angry person," through the lens of IFS you would say a part of you holds anger and sometimes takes over and acts out of anger. And this part of you feels angry because another member of your inner family was harmed. Viewing this part of you as a protective member of your inner family can open space for compassion and alleviate shame.

◦ Notice whether any of the 8 Cs (for instance, curiosity or compassion) arise as you realize that your identity is not defined by things that make you cringe. Those impulses and emotions are vital information.

- If you are curious about noticing different members of your inner family, set an intention, and see how they respond. An intention is a desire to change a behavior—to do more or less of something or react differently to circumstances. When you bring the intention to mind, notice the response of various internal family members. Some will be excited, others dubious, and some might be fearful, reluctant, or even critical. At this stage, you are acquainting yourself with various parts—just noticing who shows up and what they feel or think. I encourage you to make a note of them in your journal. Later on, you can revisit this exercise and move from awareness to connection.

Chapter Four

The Stories of Wounding That Shape Us

2 Kings 25:1-12, Lamentations

Life Under Siege

The pain of hunger woke Samara from restless sleep.[1] Her body felt leaden from nightmares filled with images of people lying dead where they collapsed from hunger. Tears rolled down her temples as she thought of the children begging for food and water in the dusty streets.[2] How long could they endure the siege? Her confidence that God's anointed king would prevail was waning.

Each day felt more challenging than the last. Weariness plagued her, and her home felt oppressive rather than welcoming. Yet, the voice inside saying, "Don't go outside!" increasingly won out over her loneliness. And why wouldn't it? When she ventured out, her suffering was magnified in the faces of everyone she saw. No one could offer comfort; everyone was preoccupied with their misery.[3]

Unbearable cruelty filled Samara with turmoil as she veered from rage over the brutality of influential people whose political games devastated lives, to

---

1. Samara is a Hebrew name meaning "protected by God." This is a fictional character experiencing the events described in 2 Kings 25:1-21, 2 Chronicles 36:17-21, Jeremiah 39:1-10, and Lamentations.

2. Lamentations 4:4-5, NRSV

3. Lamentations 1:2, NRSV

numb disbelief that the religious rulers could be so wrong about Jerusalem being invincible.[4]

As she prayed for the strength to endure another day, she was startled by loud voices outside. A wave of sound hit when she opened the door. People ran through the streets shouting, "The Babylonians breached the walls! They're pouring into the city!"[5]

Terror gripped her gut. No one would be safe now.

The next day, as the women gathered at the well for water, the worst news imaginable was whispered around the circle: "They captured the king and slaughtered his sons!"[6]

Samara felt powerless and bitter. The rulers promised to protect them, and the priests said no one could prevail over God's anointed king. Her body trembled with anxiety; thoughts about whether she would survive and what life would be like plagued her. She tried to pray and trust that God cared and was still listening, but she wondered if the Lord had abandoned his people.

The Unthinkable Happens

A few weeks later, Samara smelled smoke as she prepared a meal from her meager supplies. She climbed the ladder to the roof and saw fires everywhere. What was that vast blaze? Samara struggled to make sense of what she was seeing. The temple was burning![7] How could the Lord allow this destruction!?

Samara watched the fires raging, paralyzed with shock. The sight of soldiers dragging people from their homes jolted her out of her trance. Running inside, frantic to find a hiding place, Samara crawled under her bed, hoping they would think she had abandoned her home.

---

4. "The people were entrenched in the confidence that the Temple, city, and nation were eternally secure in Yahweh's covenant with David." *A History of Israel*, 3rd ed, John Bright, pg. 326. See Jeremiah 5:12, 7:4, 14:13.

5. Ibid, pg. 330

6. 2 Kings 25:6-7

7. 2 Kings 25:9, NRSV

When her door burst open, and she saw the soldier's boots, Samara held her breath, her heart pounding. The boots came closer, and the soldier laughed as he tossed her bed aside, pointing his sword at her and grabbing her legs. She screamed, terrified he would assault her, having heard stories of brutality at the hands of Babylonian soldiers.[8] But he just shoved her into a crowd of people, stunned into silence as they marched together through the city.

Everywhere she looked, she saw the destruction. The few people who resisted being taken captive were killed, their bodies tossed into the street.[9] Samara retched into the gutter,[10] overcome by horror.

Soldiers herded people like sheep. Swords and spears prodded them as they left the city. But could Jerusalem even be called a city anymore? Soldiers burned and looted the Temple, desecrating the sacred things, along with everything else in the city.[11]

The only home Samara had ever known was uninhabitable.[12] And as she trudged through the countryside, she realized Jerusalem was just the final chapter of the plan to destroy the last remnant of God's people. The surrounding towns and fields were utterly ruined.[13]

Life in Exile

Her knees throbbed after hours spent scrubbing the endless hallways in the palace. At least the mind-numbing work distracted her from the pain of worthlessness. God wouldn't have allowed this to happen if her life mattered—if she were lovable. She felt shame heat her face. Was she so defective and useless that God withdrew from her life?

---

8. Lamentations 5:11, NRSV

9. Lamentations 2:21, NRSV

10. Lamentations 2:11, NRSV

11. 2 Kings 25:9, NRSV, 2 Kings 25:13-17, NRSV

12. *A History of Israel,* 3rd ed, John Bright, pg. 331

13. Ibid, pg. 331

Samara felt cut off from the woman who used to sing songs celebrating God's loving care; who was she? There was no room in this painful existence for the joy she felt during festivals as she danced in the streets surrounded by family and friends. Bitterness closed her throat; she could no longer praise God. Why praise the God who rejected her, who cast her out? She wanted answers! Why do you keep forgetting us? How could you dump us in Babylon?[14]

Bitterness gave her the energy to scrub her enemy's floors, but inevitably, it gave way to despair. She rubbed her tears into the stones, watching them disappear just as her pleas for mercy vanished into the void of God's absence.

The heaviness of grief oppressed Samara more than the captors who enslaved her. She was so tired of feeling hopeless! She had no power to change her circumstances.

From deep in her soul, through layers of unanswered pain and doubt, Samara drew energy to cry out, "Restore me to you, Lord! Give me new life—unless you have utterly rejected me, and are angry with me beyond measure."[15]

The Impact of Betrayal

Samara represents the thousands of Judahites[16] exiled to Babylon following the destruction of the Temple—the most traumatic event in the history of God's people. For people who believed the Temple was the location of God's presence, in the land God promised them forever, the triumph of the pagan enemy forces was incomprehensible. The turmoil provoked serious questions: Had God forgotten the chosen people? How could God allow this devastation? Had God turned away from the covenant made at Sinai? Was God powerless in the face of Babylonian deities? Did the survivors have a future? Was there any hope of restoration?[17]

The Exile felt like a betrayal of trust.

---

14. Lamentations 5:20, The Message

15. Paraphrased from Lamentations 5:21-22, NRSV

16. At this point in Israel's history, the land had been divided into the Northern Kingdom and Southern Kingdom. Assyria conquered the Northern Kingdom in 722 BC. The people living in the Southern Kingdom—the land of Judah—were called Judahites.

17. NRSV, New Interpreter's Study Bible, pg. 1051

Betrayal of trust is at the heart of our most painful experiences. Whether you suffered trauma—abuse, assault, racism, neglect, violence—or you experienced adversity—any of myriad distressing life experiences—you felt betrayed. You trusted your parents, your coaches, and your teachers. You trusted your spouse or partner, your friends, and your pastors. You trusted that your loved ones would live long lives. You trusted political and religious systems. You trusted your employer. You trusted yourself to know whether that person was safe. You trusted your body. You trusted God that the world was a good and kind place.

Betrayal shattered that trust and your sense of safety. It disrupted your sense of self. And it altered your inner landscape.

Recall the ideal state of your internal family. You have a leader who draws on God-given resources like compassion, perspective, and confidence. Various parts of you—your inner family members—possess qualities, talents, and skills that combine to make you a uniquely wonderful person.

And then you experience betrayal.

Wherever betrayal lies on the spectrum—from feeling shamed by a parent for a mistake, to violent assault—it leaves a legacy of pain in your inner system. The part of you who experienced the adverse event carries that pain.

If a young child witnesses a verbally violent confrontation between her parents, part of her will hold distressing emotions such as terror, helplessness, and confusion. Her body contains associated sensations. The images of the conflict and beliefs about herself—"It's my fault they're arguing," "I'm not safe"—will also be stored as part of the memory of the event.

Adverse experiences burden members of the inner family with painful emotions, sensations, beliefs, and images. We feel terror, grief, shame, panic, or helplessness. Distorted beliefs, including "It's my fault," "I'm stupid," "I'm worthless," or "I'm unlovable," feel true. There are distressing images, and our body holds tension. We were wounded, and we are vulnerable to reexperiencing the pain of the wound.

We are "triggered," or activated, when we reexperience these elements of the memory. We feel distressing emotions, beliefs, images, and sensations with varying intensity. And, as you can probably attest from your own experience, normal functioning is complex when triggered. Depending on the severity of the incident, when a memory surfaces, we might be somewhat preoccupied or wholly disconnected from present reality, as we reexperience the original event.

I want to be clear that every human experiences adversity. In a landmark 1990s study, physicians surveyed a large population of over 17,000 patients enrolled in a Health Maintenance Organization (HMO) to research the effects of adverse childhood experiences (ACEs).[18] The researchers identified ten ACEs, including emotional or physical abuse, sexual abuse, emotional neglect, physical neglect, separation or divorce, witnessing domestic violence, exposure to drug or alcohol abuse, a mentally ill caregiver, and incarceration of a family member. The results showed that ACEs are far more common than previously understood. More than two-thirds of respondents reported at least one ACE, and more than one in five reported three or more ACEs. Because study participants were "mostly white, middle class, middle-aged, well-educated and financially secure enough to have good medical insurance," this was not a population previously thought to be at high risk for ACEs.[19]

According to one of the researchers who led the ACE study, the ten items represent "the tip of the iceberg" of significant stressors.[20] The death of a caregiver, prolonged illness, bullying, frequent moves, financial difficulties, lack of affection from caregivers, and discord between parents are all common examples of adversity. And these kinds of adverse events burden members of your internal family.

Adverse events span a continuum from distress to extreme forms of trauma. *Where* your experiences fall on the continuum is not as crucial as *how* they shape your inner system. One of the foremost trauma experts, Dr. Gabor Maté, says, "Trauma is not what happens to you; it's what happens inside you in response to what happens to you."[21] In my experience, the same statement applies to any distressing event. Whatever we experience, our internal system adapts to survive it.

---

18. The study was conducted by Vincent Felitti and Robert Anda at Kaiser Permanente in San Diego. See https://www.cdc.gov/violenceprevention/aces/about.html for details.

19. *The Body Keeps the Score,* Bessel van der Kolk, p. 145

20. *Childhood Disrupted: How Your Biography Becomes Your Biology, and How You Can Heal,* Donna Jackson Nakazawa, pg 25

21. https://thewisdomoftrauma.com/berlin/ Retrieved on 1/31/23

Our Internal Exiles

Because their pain can be activated, inner family members holding distressing emotions, beliefs, images, and sensations pose a risk to the system. When something stirs up pain from our past, we feel flooded and overwhelmed, or distracted and preoccupied. We are less connected to the present and more immersed in the past. This makes it difficult to function normally—a threat to our system.

Other parts of the system then exile the wounded part to contain this threat. They adopt strategies to isolate the parts holding pain—parts we call *exiles* because they are kept as far from awareness as possible. There are many creative strategies for containing exiles—for putting walls around the most vulnerable members of our inner family—and we will explore these strategies in detail in chapters six and seven. For now, I want you to understand more about your exiles.

Exiles are vulnerable, tender, and often-young members of the internal family. While we can be wounded at any age, when we connect to our exiles, we often find they are young because it is more difficult to process challenging circumstances with immature brains. And human brains take a long time to develop! From birth through at least adolescence, we are dependent on adults to help us make sense of our experiences.

Sometimes there is someone a child can turn to for support when they feel overwhelmed by things such as shame, grief, or fear. Children need to safely feel their feelings, gain perspective about their role and responsibility and reconnect with a sense of self-efficacy. When adults support a child in processing their distressing experiences, they are not left holding painful emotions and associated sensations. In the presence of a comforting adult, they can feel their feelings and receive reassurance that they are not at fault for others' choices.

No matter how well-intentioned the adults are in a child's life, this does not always happen. The younger the child is, the less likely they can communicate about the experience. A parent can understandably miss the message in a child's behavior change or dysregulated emotions. If the incident provokes shame, the child is less likely to tell anyone about it. Family culture plays a role as well. If the family rule is to "get over it," a child might believe it is not okay to share vulnerable stories. Sometimes a child's story activates the adult's wounds and they react with anger or avoidance, magnifying the child's distress. And, when parents or other family members are sources of adversity such as pain, instability, or confusion, the child might not have anyone to turn to for support.

In each scenario, painful emotions, images, sensations, and beliefs adhere to the part of us who experienced the event. This part of us becomes an exile in the inner system. Your exiles hold the stories of times you suffered pain, and they remain the age at which you experienced adversity.

We think of stories as words, as a narrative. However, memories of adverse and traumatic events *are* the sensations, images, emotions, and beliefs—the burdens held by our exiles. Sometimes we also have a narrative to make sense of all we carry. But the younger we are when the event happens—and the more traumatic it is—the more we carry information as sensations and emotions rather than words. As Janina Fisher, a leading trauma expert, says, "The symptoms tell the story better than the story."[22]

Whatever the content of our stories of suffering, these stories reflect the meaning we made of events. Because of the sensations and emotions felt during the incident, our bodies hold the message that we are not safe in the world. The inability to respond to a threat—because of an immature brain or the power the other person possesses—leaves a legacy of powerlessness that affects us physically and mentally. We can get stuck in a hypoaroused state of passivity and even collapse. Adversity often leaves a residue of shame, the painful emotion we feel when we believe we are defective—"I'm worthless," "I'm unlovable," or "I'm alone."

Often, the meaning we make of adversity lies outside of conscious awareness. Remember, internal family members diligently try to keep painful burdens from overwhelming us. We feel the echo of their presence—subtle cues in our body, flitting thoughts of worthlessness, a passing wave of grief or fear—until we are activated. And then we are back in it, back in the hours, days, or years of suffering.

Return with me to Samara's world and enter back into her misery.

Samara wept bitterly over her profound loneliness. There was no one to comfort her, no place she could safely rest. She felt naked—stripped of her humanity—worthless. In captivity, her stomach churned; she groaned over a heart

22. Janina Fisher - Complex Trauma Course (3rd video of Module 1)

wrung out by despair. Humiliation flooded her body and pulled her into the darkness, weighing her down like heavy chains. She desperately cried out to God for help but heard no response.

What if, Samara wonders, God abandoned me?

The Questions Pain Provokes

The cry of the exiles: "Restore us to yourself, Lord!" Give us new life "unless you have utterly rejected us, and are angry with us beyond measure,"[23] is our cry. Our wounded, vulnerable exiles long for reconciliation; they feel abandoned. Despair clouds their hope. They wonder if their suffering is because they have done something worthy of God's wrath. What a terrible dilemma.

Painful experiences provoke anger, doubt, hopelessness, and despair. The chaos of emotions, sensations, and beliefs reflects the activity of many members of our internal family. Some of our protective parts wonder how a personal, loving God can allow terrible things to happen. They lean into reasoning and thinking to try to make sense of tragedy. Other protectors direct their anger toward God, blaming God for failing to control things they believe God should control. Think of Job's friends trying to make sense of his suffering. They were confident Job did something to deserve punishment. "Surely God does not reject one who is blameless."[24] Sometimes, like Job's friends, a part of us is certain suffering is our fault.

In other words, parts of us work diligently to make sense of pain. They want to control and explain what feels out-of-control and inexplicable. They focus substantial energy on the question of responsibility. Who is at fault? Why did this happen? The quest for certainty underlies various theologies—it is a primary protective strategy. If I know who is responsible—me? God? Evil? Systemic oppression?—and why it happened, I can resolve it. I can regain a sense of power, which feels much better than powerlessness. These are all valid and even vital questions. But they can also be a distraction—a strategy to avoid the pain—that derails the healing process.

---

23. Lamentations 5:20 NRSV

24. Job 8:20, NIV

Our protectors want to avoid being overwhelmed by the pain our exiles hold—from the powerlessness, grief, shame, and hopelessness they carry. They have one eye on our vulnerability and the other on external forces that are the source of wounds. Imagine them as a group of very fit, muscular, well-armed protectors who believe it is up to them to stave off further attacks. They are so focused on threats that they have lost sight of our true sources of strength—our identity as God's beloved, the promise of God's unfailing love, and the presence of God in our struggles.

The most harmful effect of distressing experiences is that they make us doubt our belovedness.

Adversity instills distorted beliefs—both explicit and implicit—about our relationship with God. An explicit belief would be, "If God really loves me, that wouldn't have happened." An implicit belief is not a narrative about ourselves. It is a feeling in our bodies that we are not safe or worthy of care. It is a response in our nervous system to perceived threats that sends us into hyperarousal—fight or flight—or hypoarousal—freeze. This activity in our internal system blocks our connection to God and leaves us stranded, doubting our belovedness. As Justin McRoberts writes, believing we are beloved "is one of the most confoundingly and tragically elusive realities in human experience...because it is the thing every dark force in history most violently and vehemently seeks to distract you from and keep you from knowing."[25]

Our distressing experiences impact our internal family like a dark force invading the sacred space where Love prevails, in which we trust that God delights in us. The darkness distorts our vision of how God sees us.

Does this remind you of the story of Adam and Eve in the Garden? They lived in harmony with God and Creation, naked and unashamed.[26] I think of their nakedness as a state of complete vulnerability. There was no shame, so they did not have to hide their needs, desires, hopes, or dreams. They trusted God as a source of wisdom. And then, the dark force enters the story, tempting them to doubt

---

25. *Sacred Strides*, Justin McRoberts, pg. 13

26. Genesis 2:25

God's care for them.[27] Our earliest sacred story is an effort to explain what we all experience to some degree: a rupture in our intimate connection with God.

Am I suggesting that a dark force still operates in this world and that there is more to the story of suffering than a focus on individual sin indicates? Yes, *and* ultimately, what matters most is that we heal anything that blocks our ability to believe we are beloved.

We can get sidetracked by intriguing but complex questions about the origins of evil and whether biblical accounts about evil—the tempter, the accuser, the father of lies—are just antiquated efforts to explain what we now see as physical or mental illness or personal sin. The *origin* of evil is a question with either no answer or many answers—much to the dismay of our protectors, who believe unlocking that mystery is the key to our dilemma.

While the origin remains a mystery, the *activity* prompted by evil is evident. Renowned New Testament scholar N.T. Wright says, "Jesus [defined] the battle which had to be fought as the battle against the real enemy, the accuser, the satan."[28] Jesus "renounced the battle that his contemporaries expected a Messiah to fight. He faced, instead...the battle against the forces of darkness, standing behind the visible forces [both religious and political] ranged against him."[29] Our inner family members—both protectors and exiles—need to know that *"The earliest Christians regarded Jesus' achievement on the cross as the decisive victory over evil."*[30]

"Then why does evil still seem to have free reign in the world?" one might ask. This is another question to which there are many answers. And it's another question that takes us down a rabbit trail leading away from healing. I am not trying to conveniently dodge the question. I recommend delving into it if it is a persistent concern for you. Yet, I want you to know recovery does not *require* answers. Spending time with the part of you who wrestles with the question and wants answers might be necessary as a step on your journey. But, often, it is not

---

27. Genesis 3:1

28. N.T. Wright, The Reasons for Jesus' Crucifixion, in Brad Jersak and Michael Hardin (ed.s), *Stricken by God?* Pg. 143

29. Ibid, pg. 143

30. Ibid, pg. 145

answers that soothe our protectors. It is the reassurance that the Presence of Love can heal our pain. That is their chief concern because pain is the threat that drives their actions.

Jesus' Answer for Pain

Jesus answered the question of pain with *presence.*

Imagine Jesus speaking the words of Luke 4—good news, freedom, favor—to your exiles, promising deliverance, recovery, and reinstatement as one God sees and loves. Jesus' ministry—the whole story from the beginning to the resurrection—is "the historical and concrete acting out of [God's] promise to defeat evil and rescue people from exile."[31] Parts of you live in exile longing for *shalom*—for wholeness and peace—and the Spirit works even as you read these words to guide you back to the truth[32] of your belovedness.

Jesus' ministry reflects his mission to rescue people from exile. Recall the story of the bleeding woman we read in chapter one. Her ailment exiled her from the human community because she was considered unclean.

Matthew, the tax collector—a person reviled among Jews as a sinner—was invited to be one of Jesus' closest friends.[33] Jesus accepted people categorized as sinners; they were welcomed and told the kingdom of God belonged to them as much as anyone.

One of the first people to hear Jesus call himself Messiah was a Samaritan woman[34]—someone faithful Jews shunned. While we do not know why she was married five times, nor do we know the nature of the relationship with the man with whom she currently lived, Jesus did not rebuke her. His comment indicates that he knew her story, and he honored her by sharing part of his story with her. Jesus revealed the truth about his identity to her that not even his closest disciples knew at the time.

---

31. N.T. Wright, The Reasons for Jesus' Crucifixion, in Brad Jersak and Michael Hardin (ed.s), *Stricken by God?* Pg. 141

32. John 16:13, NIV

33. Matthew 9:9-13, Mark 2:13-17, Luke 5:27-28 NIV

34. John 4:4-26, NIV

Crowds full of people living under the tyranny of Roman rule—political and economic exile—followed Jesus to learn about the kingdom of God that the Apostle Paul later described as one where "there is neither Jew nor Gentile, neither slave nor free, nor is there male and female, for you are all one in Christ Jesus."[35] The categories used to exile people from an intimate relationship with God, from enjoying their identity as beloved, dissolved in the community Jesus established.

Jesus reveals his heart for exiles in the parables of the lost in Luke 15. A shepherd leaves his flock to find one lost sheep—joyfully putting it on his shoulders to carry it home. Then he throws a party so everyone can rejoice with him.[36] The widow who loses one coin searches diligently until she finds it and invites her community to share the joy of restoring her treasured possession.[37] And in the parable that reveals the depth of Jesus' unconditional love, the father eagerly welcomes both a son who sinned egregiously and a son who obeyed out of duty, not love.[38] Once again, a joyful celebration marks the return of the "lost" beloved. In each parable, Jesus casts a vision for restoring the lost to full participation in family and community.

Sadly, some in the Church have used the idea of "lost" people to define rigid boundaries of who is inside and outside God's favor. Yet, Jesus tells these stories to demonstrate his passion for welcoming everyone—restoring everyone to being safe, seen, soothed, and secure[39] —because we are—*you* are—beloved.

Jesus' mission "to seek and save the lost"—to rescue exiles—infuses hope in our internal family.[40] It is an example from which we learn how to respond to our inner exiles. We become what Dr. Schwartz calls "hope-merchants," a source of hope for hurting internal family members. Hope opens the door to possibility. Hope energizes the painstaking process of connecting with your protectors and

---

35. Galatians 3:28, NIV

36. Luke 15:4-6, NIV

37. Luke 15:8-9, NIV

38. Luke 15:11-32, NIV

39. *Parenting from the Inside Out,* Daniel J. Siegel & Mary Hartzell, pg. 108

40. Luke 19:10, NIV

exiles to restore relationships broken by experiences beyond your control. Hope fuels the journey to *shalom.*

Spiritual Practice: Exploring the Impact of Adversity on Your Internal Family

What is your response to the word "hope?" It might range from fear of embracing the possibility of change to cautious optimism to elation.

- Accept whatever you notice as a valid response from your internal system.
- Parts of you might be concerned about the vulnerability of hope; after all, if you allow yourself to hope, you might be disappointed. Your response to hope helps you learn vital information about your internal system for your healing journey.

Imagine Jesus speaking the words of his mission to *you. "The Spirit of the Lord is on me, because he has anointed me to proclaim good news to the poor. He has sent me to proclaim freedom for the prisoners and recovery of sight for the blind, to set the oppressed free, to proclaim the year of the Lord's favor."* Read them slowly and notice if a particular phrase resonates. How does it feel in your body as Jesus speaks these words to you? If it feels meaningful, write these verses in your journal.

As you read about the inevitable experience and impact of adversity, did any of your own experiences come to mind? Perhaps you identified an exiled member of your internal family. Later in the book, we will cover the healing steps used with exiles. For now, just imagine connecting with this vulnerable part of you. Notice whether you feel compassion for their experience. Healing happens through the relationship between the Self, Spirit, and members of the inner family. Let them know you are aware of them, are sorry for their pain, and intend to help them heal.

- Each time you connect with a member of your internal family, you establish and strengthen a relationship. Use your journal to track connections with inner family members; recording this interaction will help you honor your commitment to them.

Often, recalling difficult experiences provokes grief. No matter the nature of the events, they involve loss—loss of dreams, trust, safety, security, etc.

- When sadness wells up, what happens inside?
    - Do you notice any part(s) who distract you?
    - Do you hear from parts who think sadness is "weak" or frightening?
    - If you feel persistent resistance to allowing grief to surface, honor it. Parts who are concerned about grief should not be ignored. You will learn the practice of connecting with them. For now, extend gratitude for their presence.

At this stage of the process, the goal is to notice whatever arises and whether you feel the presence of Self and Spirit. Pushing past parts of the system who hold concerns is never helpful.

- If it feels safe, practice allowing the wave of sadness to well up and dissipate. Can you be patient with the flow of emotions through your body?
- Your history of loss will affect your inner system's response to grief, particularly if you have not had the opportunity to process it. Please attend to your inner wisdom; if parts of you are unwilling to allow space for grief, thank them for their desire to protect you. You might need the support of a therapist to work with grief.[41]
- If other emotions arise, practice being with the parts holding them. Notice whether you feel confident, calm, curious, courageous, or

---

41. You can search for an IFS therapist in your area through the IFS Institute website: https://ifs-institute.com/practitioners

compassionate.

- If you don't notice any C qualities, that's okay! Or, if you notice just a wee bit of Self-energy, that's okay too. Everyone's inner family is unique, and if you have experienced significant adversity or trauma, it will likely take time to release constraints to healing resources.

- Note any significant experiences, insights, or connections with members of your internal family.

Chapter Five

Stories Live in Our Bodies

Luke 13:10-17

The searing jolt of pain startled Leah out of deep sleep.[1] Some mornings, a part of her forgot the cost of attempting to stretch her spine. Tears slid down her temple as she brought her knees to her chest in a futile attempt to ease the spasm in her back. Eyes closed, Leah grasped at the tendrils of a fleeting dream where she lay flat, arms and legs outstretched, and face turned to the sun in a field of wildflowers. But she couldn't hold onto it; the dream did not withstand the searing heat in her body.

How could part of her imagine feeling free after so many years of pain? She slipped from the field of flowers back to the awful season of loss, where her body first registered the weight of grief.

Leah's parents loved to tell the story of her name. The sixth of their children, they named her Leah with confidence that she—like Jacob's wife—would have many children. Leah never doubted how her life would unfold—that it would look like the other women in her extended family. But each time she got pregnant, she lost the baby. Leah never felt free to grieve; trusting God meant focusing on the hope that next time she would carry the baby to term. Her stomach clenched when she felt the familiar cramps; her heart raced, knowing what lay ahead. Her mother's penetrating gaze registered as an accusation, tensing her muscles for the fight over what she was doing wrong and how she disgraced the family.

As the years passed and the losses mounted, she felt more rigidity in her body. Her breath caught in her throat as prickly sensations radiated from her neck down her arms to her fingers. On bad days, pain pulsed in hot flashes down her spine. The unrelenting assault of experiences on her body gradually caused her to fold over to protect her tenderness. And now she couldn't stand up straight. Simple

---

1. Leah is my name for the woman in Luke 13:10-17.

tasks sent waves of discomfort throughout her body, filling her with shame for being so broken.

The more her body showed the effect of her grief and shame, the more disconnected she felt. Her husband was dutiful but distant, and her parents insisted she should trust God's will for her to be a mother. They wondered aloud what she might have done to deserve barrenness, and if they caught her crying, they chastised her for her lack of faith. Women in her village looked at her with pity. Loneliness crushed her heart, and relationships didn't feel safe. The emotions constantly swirling inside were overwhelming, sending her into a downward spiral of hopelessness. Her body sometimes collapsed under the weight of despair.

Gradually, her attention returned to the present—to the familiar tug and pull of dread and duty. Part of her wanted to stay in bed and sink into the futility of living this life. Turning her face into her pillow to quiet her sobs, she gave in to grief. The spasm in her back eased, replaced by a dull ache, and she got up to prepare for Sabbath services.

Leah slipped into the synagogue as late as possible, sitting in the back to avoid stares. There was always someone startled and disgusted by her tortured body. When the visiting teacher called her forward, panic washed over her. Would he call out her faithlessness and sin as deserving of God's judgment? Heart pounding, she clenched her teeth and forced her constricted muscles to move. Every step forward was torture; shame flooded her body as she anticipated his rebuke.

Jesus tenderly said, "Woman, you are set free from your infirmity."[2]

She looked into eyes brimming with tears, and compassion flooded her body. Like blood flowing to every cell, healing energy released tendons and fibers from captivity. Rigid muscles softened, and she breathed deeply for the first time in years. Leah lifted her head and straightened her spine. Spacious calm replaced searing pain. Confidence in her worth rose from her soul, healing her shame. Favorite verses welled up:

> Praise the Lord, my soul;
> all my inmost being praise his holy name.
> Praise the Lord, my soul,
> and forget not all his benefits—

---

2. Luke 13:12, NIV

who forgives all your sins
and heals all your diseases,
who redeems your life from the pit
and crowns you with love and compassion,
who satisfies your desires with good things
so that your youth is renewed like the eagle's.[3]

Then the synagogue leader indignantly protested Jesus healing on the Sabbath,[4] and the sacred moment they had shared evaporated. Would the people turn on her as well? The old fear began to creep back into her bones.

But Jesus spoke words that freed her from the last of her distress. "You hypocrites! Doesn't each of you on the Sabbath untie your ox or donkey from the stall and lead it out to give it water? Then should not this woman, a daughter of Abraham, whom Satan has kept bound for eighteen long years, be set free on the Sabbath day from what bound her?"[5]

While the leaders grumbled, family and friends surrounded Leah, rejoicing over her healing.

Our Bodies Hold Our Experiences

The Gospels record many stories of healing. Yet, most do not identify a "spirit" as the cause of infirmity, nor does Jesus routinely speak of Satan as the culprit. In the story of the "crippled woman" healed on the Sabbath, however, Luke writes, "On a Sabbath Jesus was teaching in one of the synagogues, and a woman was there who had been crippled *by a spirit* for eighteen years" (italics mine).[6] Jesus called religious leaders who protested about healing on the Sabbath hypocrites for not wanting this woman to be "set free" from Satan's bondage.[7] His focus was not

---

3. Psalm 103:1-5, NIV

4. Luke 13:14, NIV

5. Luke 13:15-16, NIV

6. Luke 13:10, NIV

7. Luke 13:16, NIV

just her physical symptoms, devastating as those were; in this encounter, Jesus was clearly freeing the oppressed.[8]

Jesus blurs the boundaries between the physical and spiritual realms in this story of redemption. He challenges religious leaders to look beyond legalistic practices that close their eyes to oppression. In elevating the suffering woman's needs over religiosity, Jesus invites people into the kingdom where God is present and working to restore wholeness. It is an expansive and redemptive moment.

But what are we to make of Jesus pointing to Satan's influence over the woman? How are we to understand a story like this in our modern context? Typically, we assume ignorance of the disease process led ancient people to attribute illness to dark forces.

Perhaps the ancient view deserves respect instead of dismissal. We now know that there is a dose-response relationship between adversity and both physical and mental illness—the more adversity we experience, the worse our physical and mental health status.[9] While we do not tend to label loss, abuse, addiction, and myriad other common causes of distress "evil," they are, aren't they? Don't these devastating experiences wreak havoc on lives? They do, and our bodies hold their effects. And we wonder—as the woman must have—if God cares.

God does care. "When Jesus saw her, he called her forward."[10] Jesus saw a woman who was "socially invisible."[11] He didn't see her physical ailment alone; he knew what it cost her emotionally because he understood their culture. The woman healed by Jesus lived in an honor and shame culture, where honor "was the public affirmation of a person's value by his or her peers" and shame was "the lack

---

8. *The New International Commentary on the New Testament: The Gospel of Luke*, Joel B. Green, pg. 522 referring to Luke 4:18-19

9. This correlation was discovered in the ACE study conducted by Vincent Felitti and Robert Anda at Kaiser Permanente in San Diego. See https://www.cdc.gov/violenceprevention/aces/about.html for details.

10. Luke 13:12, NIV

11. *The New International Commentary on the New Testament: The Gospel of Luke*, Joel B. Green, pg. 522

or loss of honor due to one's social position."[12] Her condition would place her among the "destitute" in her society, the lowest tier of a stratified community.[13] Jesus saw her *and* the system she was embedded in—the religious and social forces that cast her to the margins.

Whatever the cause of the woman's disability, social shame magnified the effect, and her body carried it. Being shamed for conditions beyond our control is a manifestation of evil. It is a source of oppression, and Jesus came to free the oppressed.[14] Jesus' loving compassion enabled him to "feel with" the woman—to sense the emotional pain coursing through her body. Curt Thompson, a psychiatrist who integrates neuroscience and Christianity, writes shame "is both a source and result of evil's active assault on God's creation."[15] It breaks connection at a time when a connection is vital, and it reinforces distorted beliefs of worthlessness.

The woman's bowed back told a story that Jesus shared—a story of the struggle between God's desire for flourishing and the impact of evil in this world. In naming Satan as her oppressor—the one who "kept her bound for eighteen long years"[16] —Jesus put her story in the broader context of his ministry to proclaim God's kingdom where goodness prevails over evil—where the oppressed are set free. This is not a place you go when you die. It is a here-and-now, embodied reality of God's presence with and for all.

This ancient story illustrates what science has since uncovered: the body keeps the score.[17] We now know "mind and body are inseparable...and illness and health cannot be understood in isolation from life histories, social context, and emotional

---

12. *The New Testament in its World: An Introduction to the History, Literature, and Theology of the First Christians,* N.T. Wright and Michael F. Bird, pg. 114

13. Ibid, pg 111

14. Luke 4:18-19

15. *The Soul of Shame: Retelling the Stories We Believe About Ourselves,* Curt Thompson, MD, pg. 13

16. Luke 13:16, NIV

17. *The Body Keeps the Score: Brain, Mind, and Body in the Healing of Trauma,* Bessel van der Kolk, p. 86

patterns."[18] This is why it is essential to cultivate awareness of our bodies on our journey to *shalom.* In a culture where we privilege cognition—beliefs, knowledge, and rationality—the body is not always considered a source of wisdom. But our bodies hold our stories, *and* they manifest the impact of those stories. Connecting with our bodies helps us connect with the stories held by our internal family members. And ultimately, as we witness those stories, we participate in Jesus' mission too—freeing the oppressed.

How the Body Keeps the Score

Understanding some basic physiology is crucial for cultivating awareness of the language our bodies speak. Sometimes when we connect with parts of us, they will share a narrative; more commonly however, especially initially, they will communicate through sensations in our bodies.

Think of your body as a sacred container of interconnected systems that grow and constantly change in response to your environment. One of those systems—our central nervous system—plays a significant role in capturing our stories and informing us about their effect.

Dr. Curt Thompson writes, "The central nervous system includes the brain and spinal cord, yet neuroscientists also speak of the extended brain. This refers to the brain's connections, via cranial and peripheral nerves, to other organs, most notably the viscera (the heart, lungs, and the digestive tract).[19]

Imagine the energy of emotion—the primary language parts of us speak—traveling from deep in your core—your chest and gut—out through your spine and into your limbs. Recall an emotionally charged memory—joyful, sorrowful, or fearful. Can you feel the memory traveling through your body? Maybe it is most prominent in one location. While the brain allows us to recall words and images, we *feel* stories as they warm our hearts, constrict our chests, alter our breathing, or clench our bellies. Our nervous system lights up when we recollect an impactful story. It's like a house covered in Christmas lights; the picture emerges as each set of lights is plugged in.

---

18. *When the Body Says No: Exploring the Stress Disease Connection,* Gabor Maté

19. *Anatomy of the Soul: Surprising Connections Between Neuroscience and Spiritual Practices That Can Transform Your Life and Relationships,* Curt Thompson, MD, pg. 42

Our stories are not discrete chapters in the book of our lives; they are interconnected. Because of how our minds develop, we experience them as the interplay of our earliest life experiences with the present moment.

Our brains cluster early experiences into "mental models" that help us efficiently "interpret present experiences [and] anticipate future ones."[20] These mental models—symbolic stories of early experiences—operate outside of conscious awareness, so we do not realize how our past experiences bias our perception of present experiences. These implicit (nonconscious) memories "come in the form of perceptions, behaviors, emotions, and bodily experiences" and are "often revealed through nonverbal communication and body language."[21]

Awareness of the sometimes subtle ways our body communicates can facilitate connection with the parts of us holding stories containing unresolved distress—whether from past or more recent experiences. As psychologist Hillary McBride writes, "Our bodies are telling the stories we have avoided or forgotten how to hear."[22] They tell us these stories through sensation, impulse, posture, and facial expression—all of which reflect the activity of different internal family members.

The sacred container that is your body is highly permeable to its surroundings. Just as it speaks the language of sensation, impulse, posture, and expression, it *listens* to those cues in the environment. Using our senses—visual, auditory, olfactory, tactile—our bodies attune to the environment to assess safety. A smell can trigger a pleasant or unpleasant memory, impacting your sense of security. Similarly, body language, facial expressions, and tone of voice are cues your body "listens to" as it continuously monitors the environment.

Safety is the most basic need upon which our well-being rests. While each individual's definition of safety is subjective and dependent on their temperament, personality, experiences, etc., we share the need for connection—and safety is the

---

20. *The Developing Mind: How Relationships and the Brain Interact to Shape Who We Are (2nd. ed.),* Daniel J. Siegel, pg. 52

21. *Anatomy of the Soul: Surprising Connections Between Neuroscience and Spiritual Practices That Can Transform Your Life and Relationships,* Curt Thompson, MD, pg. 68

22. *The Wisdom of Your Body,* Hillary McBride, pg. 23

prerequisite to connection. When we listen to our bodies, they will tell us—loud and clear—whether they feel safe. Prickly skin, a thumping heart, a tight gut, and shallow breath indicate perceived risk. Spacious heart space, calm breath, and relaxed muscles tell you your body senses safety. These shifting states reflect the activity of your autonomic nervous system (ANS).

The ANS is the safety monitor in our bodies. Our most crucial biological task is survival, and our ANS is exquisitely capable of assessing risk and adapting to it. Understanding the structure of the ANS helps build awareness of its activity—and the activity of our internal family members.

Dr. Steven Porges transformed our understanding of the ANS with his "polyvagal theory." He discovered that our ANS has three circuits "providing adaptive responses to safe, dangerous, and life-threatening events and contexts."[23] Each of the three pathways has unique patterns of response to the environment: "the dorsal vagus (immobilization), the sympathetic nervous system (mobilization), and the ventral vagus (social engagement and connection)."[24]

Immobilization is the freeze response, while mobilization is the fight or flight response. The sympathetic nervous system mobilizes us to fight the threat or flee from it. If those strategies don't resolve the threat, the parasympathetic system protects us through freeze responses such as collapse or dissociation (disconnection). The new contribution of the polyvagal theory is the understanding that we also have a social engagement system—a branch of the ANS that supports connection with others—the state we are in when we feel safe.

Deb Dana—who brought the polyvagal theory into clinical practice—conceptualizes the branches of the ANS as a ladder where the top of the ladder is our ventral vagal state: safe, attuned, connected, and emotionally regulated.[25] Called our "social engagement" system, it is linked to "eye gaze, facial

---

23. Stephen W. Porges, "The Polyvagal Theory: New insights into adaptive reactions of the autonomic nervous system, Clev Clin J Med. 2009 april; 76 (Suppl 2): S86-S90. Doi: 10.3949/ccjm.76.s2.17 https://www.ncbi.nlm.nih.gov/pmc/articles/PMC3108032/pdf/nihms-299331.pdf pg. 3

24. *The Polyvagal Theory in Therapy: Engaging the Rhythm of Regulation,* Deb Dana, pg. 4

25. Ibid, pg. 10

expression, listening, and prosody" [tone of voice].[26] Think of how crucial these qualities are for connecting with others: eye contact, a welcoming expression, attuned ears, and a calm tone all signal safety. When the Self leads the inner family, you are in a state of social engagement.

When our bodies register a threat—when something distressing happens—our first strategy is to secure the connection that will soothe our concerns, supported by our social engagement system. External relationships are vital; consider how often you reach for a loved one to process problems. And we can also cultivate relationships between the leader of the internal family—Self—and the parts of the system who react to threats. When we attend to the signals our body sends, we can turn to the distressed part who is afraid, lonely, or ashamed and give them the assistance they need to navigate the situation.

If we don't get the support we need—because parts of us who are fearful block Self-leadership and no one else is available—the next step on the ladder is our sympathetic nervous system which mobilizes us to respond to the threat. The primary responses are fight or flight, both of which enlist various systems in our body. The endocrine system supplies adrenaline that increases heart and respiratory rates. We feel tension in our muscles and the impulse to move or strike. Senses are heightened; we scan the environment for sights and sounds. Protective parts of us decide, "The world is a dangerous place, and I need to protect myself from harm."[27]

When mobilization doesn't resolve the threat, our dorsal vagal response is immobilization or collapse. Collapse can be a protective response to a threat; when an experience is utterly overwhelming, dissociation—completely disconnecting from the present moment—enables us to survive. It can also be the chronic condition of our burdened exiles. Deb Dana describes the dorsal vagal response as "the very bottom of the autonomic ladder [where] I am alone with my despair and escape into not knowing, not feeling, almost a sense of not being...I might describe myself as hopeless, abandoned...and the world as empty, dead, and

---

26. Stephen W. Porges, "The Polyvagal Theory: New insights into adaptive reactions of the autonomic nervous system, Clev Clin J Med. 2009 april; 76 (Suppl 2): S86-S90. Doi: 10.3949/ccjm.76.s2.17 https://www.ncbi.nlm.nih.gov/pmc/articles/PMC3108032/pdf/nihms-299331.pdf pg. 4

27. *The Polyvagal Theory in Therapy: Engaging the Rhythm of Regulation,* Deb Dana, pg. 11

dark."[28] Immobilization is the bottom of the autonomic ladder *and* the basement of our internal family home, where our most vulnerable parts are locked away to keep the wider system protected from their pain.

Therapist Pete Walker suggests another immobilization strategy: the "fawn" response.[29] He noticed that clients who experienced trauma learn not to protest because that elicits punishment. Instead, they opt for being helpful, disconnecting from their needs to focus on meeting others' needs. "Servitude, ingratiation, and forfeiture of any needs that might inconvenience and ire the parent become the most important survival strategies available."[30] It is a submissive stance designed to mitigate threats and an adaptive strategy we will feel in our bodies. Typically learned in childhood, it can become a dominant protective strategy across many relationships, blocking the clarity the Self brings to determine healthy boundaries.

The branches of the vagus nerve correspond to the activity of members of our internal family. When we feel safe, the Self leads the inner family, and we feel calm, curious, and connected to ourselves and others. Under threat—real or perceived—protectors mobilize us for action through a variety of adaptive strategies—two of which are fight or flight. If the danger persists, protectors immobilize the system through methods such as dissociation and numbing. Think of exiles—who hold burdens of our most painful experiences—existing in an extended state of immobilization, burdened by hopelessness, loneliness, and despair. Through attuning to our autonomic nervous system, we learn how our body reflects our parts' presence—how they work to protect us, and the burdens they bear.

Listening to the Language of Your Body

The activity of our ANS and the neural pathways connected to our heart, lungs, and belly provide valuable clues about our inner world *and* how experiences shaped it and affect it in the present. Our goal is to use this data to enhance

---

28. Ibid, pg. 12

29. Pete Walker, http://www.pete-walker.com/codependencyFawnResponse.htm retrieved on 3/7/23

30. Ibid. pg 2

awareness of our internal family members, because awareness creates space for connection. With awareness, we shift from a blended state where reactivity constrains the influence of both Self and Spirit to a more spacious state of compassion and curiosity. Turning attention to the places in our body holding tension—our brow, throat, shoulders, chest, belly, or limbs—sends the message to parts of us that we are present, available, and interested. Tension conveys need—the need for reassurance, assistance, or response. Our attention says, "I'm here for you. I'm interested in your needs and have resources to help."

As I cast a vision for befriending your body, I recognize that bringing awareness to your body might feel unsafe. Bodies carry the impact of adversity. When your body has been the focus of mistreatment—racism, assault, objectification, or neglect—you will have protectors who use distraction, dissociation, criticism, and numerous other strategies to disconnect you from it. They are diligent because they are afraid. Yet, healing requires becoming familiar with and befriending sensations in our bodies.[31] You can remind your scared protectors that God chose your body as a dwelling place. Your body—with its unique history of anguish and awe—is a *temple* where the Spirit makes her home.[32] Your body does not repulse the Spirit; she loves every part of it.

For this profound truth to sink from head to heart, you must develop relationships with the parts of you who have learned to disconnect you from your body to keep you safe. Your breath is a bridge from distress to connection. "Slowing and deepening the breath during moments of distress brings a return of ventral vagal control, and, as our autonomic state changes, so can our story."[33] "Ventral vagal control" is where the Self leads your inner family. Slow, deep breath reassures your internal family members that it is safe to connect with your body; it orients your body to the present. And it creates space for the Self to communicate with whoever needs attention.

---

31. *The Body Keeps the Score: Brain, Mind, and Body in the Healing of Trauma,* Bessell van der Kolk, pg. 100

32. 1 Corinthians 6:19, NIV. I chose the feminine pronoun because, while I believe God transcends human gender, it can be helpful to vary pronouns, particularly if parts have had complex relationships with men and/or patriarchy.

33. *The Polyvagal Theory in Therapy: Engaging the Rhythm of Regulation,* Deb Dana,pg. 135

Think about how difficult it is to converse with someone too close to you. As you breathe in, let parts of you know you want to create space to connect with them. Breath is a God-given resource for reassuring our scared and wounded inner family members that *they are not alone.*

When Jesus appeared to the disciples after his resurrection, "he breathed on them and said, 'Receive the Holy Spirit.'"[34] Breath connects us to God through the Spirit. In the creation story, humanity came alive when God breathed the breath of life into them.[35] Psalm 104:30 says, "When you send your Spirit, [all creatures] are created."[36] Breath carries the Spirit into our bodies, bringing life-giving energy that restores and redeems brokenness.

Using your breath to calm your inner system facilitates awareness. After taking several long, slow breaths, ask, "What is my body telling me?" Parts use your body to let you know how they feel,[37] and as you practice awareness, they will increasingly trust that you are listening. Information—prickly sensations running down your arms, rapid and shallow breathing, flushed cheeks, or a fast heart rate—signals the leader of the inner family that someone needs attention. Awareness moves us from "a state of 'being in' to 'being with' and brings observer energy to interrupt ingrained response pathways."[38] The Self is the observer who brings God-given resources such as perspective, clarity, and connection to protectors and exiles locked in patterns of reactivity.

Remember, our ANS is picking up environmental cues, and we interpret cues based on the stories we hold. Our reactivity often reflects stories from long ago—stories we might not be consciously aware of—more than the present moment. Parts of us are caught in a time and place where we *weren't* safe. But that was then, and this is now. When we are "in" a reactive state—either the heightened arousal of fight-or-flight or the collapsed state of fawning or numbness—Self can

---

34. John 20:22 NIV

35. Genesis 2:7

36. Psalm 104:30, NIV

37. *Somatic Internal Family Systems Therapy: Awareness, Breath, Resonance, Movement, and Touch in Practice,* Susan McConnell, pg. 67

38. *The Polyvagal Theory in Therapy: Engaging the Rhythm of Regulation,* Deb Dana, pg. 42

be "with" those parts to reassure them that they are safe. Connection with the Self brings parts into the present moment from a past filled with pain or a future they fear. Differentiating past from present facilitates safety and builds a trusting relationship.

Because our primary biological imperative is survival, our bodies—through our exquisite nervous system—are experts at detecting threats. Seen through the lens of IFS, parts in protective roles are inner family members dedicated to assessing and responding to threats. As we learn to listen to our bodies, we will often encounter protectors who assume a variety of adaptive strategies to support survival. Learning their stories is our next step on the journey to *shalom.*

Spiritual Practice: Listening to Your Body

Using your breath to calm your inner system facilitates awareness of the present moment because slow, deep breaths communicate safety to your autonomic nervous system—to your internal family members. When we listen to our bodies, they will tell us—loud and clear—whether they feel safe. Prickly skin, a thumping heart, a tight gut, and shallow breath indicate perceived risk. Spacious heart space, calm breath, and relaxed muscles tell you your body senses safety.

Making notes in your journal as you experiment with these practices will be a helpful way to learn more about the wisdom of your body. If you find this practice especially difficult to do, don't force yourself through it; listen to the current limits of your body and move at your body's pace. Some people find it helpful to breathe alongside another Self-led person, whose ventral vagal energy of social engagement can support yours.

- Turn your attention inside and ask, "What is my body telling me?" Notice whether there's an indication that any part of you does not feel safe.

- Your body "speaks" the language of sensation, posture, facial expression, muscle tone, etc. What can you notice in your body at this moment?

- Awareness moves us from a state of *being in* to *being with*. For example, when your body is riddled with anxiety, you are caught up in the storm of sensations. Your breath helps ease the intensity so you can bring loving kindness to the anxious parts of you.

- Focus on an area of your body sharing something, such as agitation, worry, or grief. Breathe deeply, and inhale slowly. Imagine your breath carrying loving kindness to the part(s) of you who are using your body to get your attention.

- As you inhale and exhale, imagine the Spirit gently touching each part of you with tenderness and love.

Another way to bring awareness and curiosity to your body is by scanning your body, starting with the top of your head and gradually shifting your attention down through your face, neck, shoulders, chest, abdomen, pelvis, and limbs. If it feels overwhelming to scan your whole body, you can notice your three centers of intelligence—head, heart, and gut.[39]

- Pause your scan when you notice tension, constriction, throbbing, or fatigue, and remain focused on the sensation if possible. You could even put a hand there in gentle support.

- If you notice a reaction to the sensation—elevated heart rate, tension elsewhere in your body, or a thought about it not being safe to focus—turn your attention to the part of you reacting. Thank them for how they are working to protect you. Invite them to be with you, breathing together, so they can feel your presence. When they relax, return your focus to the original sensation.

- If you feel curious and open to connecting, just be with the sensation. Parts of you might tell stories about it or try to figure out why it's there;

---

39. My orientation to the centers of intelligence has been through the Enneagram, a personality typology.

let them know you appreciate their help, and ask them to let you be with the sensation.

- As you attend to the sensation, notice whether there's an emotion associated with it. Can you be with it without needing it to change?
- Is there information associated with the sensation? For example, is your body telling you it's hungry, tired, overwhelmed, sad, etc?
- Notice the sensation now that you've spent time focusing on it. Often, parts relax when we focus on them because they are getting the attention they need. If a sensation intensifies with focus, use your breath to bring calm. The goal is not to use the breath to stifle sensation but to create more space for connection.

For some, especially those who have strong feelings that they may struggle to put into words, accessing emotions directly is a way to access our bodies. Imagine the energy of emotion—the primary language parts of us speak—traveling from deep in your core—your chest and gut—out through your spine and into your limbs. Recall an emotionally charged memory—joyful, sorrowful, or fearful.

- Can you feel the memory traveling through your body?
- Perhaps you feel sympathetic arousal—an impulse to fight or flee.
- Or, the memory provokes your parasympathetic response—you feel numb, frozen, or slumped.
- Bring the awareness of Self to whatever you are noticing. Let it know you are with them, and just be present, breathing gently and deeply to create a space to hold the emotion.

Your body is fascinating and incredible—the chosen home of the Holy Spirit. Cultivating an appreciation for the extraordinary wonder of your unique presence in the world requires intention and practice because it is counter-cultural to focus on what your body does well rather than on its "flaws." Bringing loving attention to your body is vital in connecting with your inner family.

- Breathe in, creating space for your confidence to well up. (Remember, confidence is a God-given resource, one of the Cs of Self-energy, so it's already in your system!)
- What part of your body can you celebrate today?
    - The legs that carry you?
    - The eyes that see God's creation?
    - The nose that smells the scents of nature?
    - The hands that play an instrument?
    - The heart that pumps faithfully?
    - The scars that testify to your resilience?
    - The autonomic nervous system that alerts you to danger and adapts to keep you safe?
    - The wrinkles, creases, and grey hairs that reflect your years of striving and surviving, of learning and maturing?
    - The places that hold the strength that defies all odds?
- If you feel resistance to celebrating your body, breathe in to create space for compassion to flow to those feelings. Parts of us hear messages about what is acceptable, and they are afraid someone will criticize us if we fall short of some ideal standard. Thank them for how they are trying to help you and offer them one example of how magnificent your body is.

Chapter Six

Protecting Ourselves from Vulnerable Stories

Excerpts from Exodus

The mixed emotions swirling through his body were confusing and disorienting. Reuben[1] longed to regain the powerful sensation of the Israelite's triumph over Pharaoh's army. Escaping enslavement and the only life he had ever known fulfilled a dream he rarely contemplated during his bitter years of labor.[2]

In the hours and days after their rescue, Reuben looked at his wife and children to ground himself in the new reality; it seemed impossible they were free from their ruthless masters. He was elated; God had delivered them!

But now, despair threatened to overwhelm his newfound sense of possibility. His jaw clenched, and his chest tightened as anger welled up. How could God save them only to send them into the desert to die? Three days and no water to slake their thirst.[3] Reuben feared his children would not survive. A growing sense of panic pushed out the last of his joy.

Reuben heard shouts from the edge of the group, "Trees! We see trees! There must be water ahead!" His panic ebbed when he, too, saw the grove of palms.[4] His muscles trembled with leftover adrenaline. Reuben was exhausted, and tears of relief pooled in his eyes. Praising God for his mercy, he quickly wiped them away so his family wouldn't see them.

---

1. Reuben is a fictional character.

2. Exodus 1:11-14, NIV

3. Exodus 15:22

4. Exodus 15:27

It was a relief to camp at the oasis for a few weeks. When the command came from the leaders to head back into the desert, Reuben felt the familiar fear for his family bubbling up inside.

Within days, his fears were justified as food began to run low. His belly rumbled with hunger, and his heart clenched with grief over not being able to feed his children.

Glancing at his wife, Reuben saw her stumble with fatigue. He was so tired of being powerless to help his family! What kind of life was this? Maybe they would have been better off staying in Egypt. At least they had food there![5] Reuben devised plans and strategies, one after the other, desperately trying to figure out how to ensure his family survived.

Anger began to build like a fire stoked by a smoldering stick. The heat spread from Reuben's chest to his limbs, consuming trust and faith, compelling action. These so-called leaders needed to answer for his family's suffering! Reuben charged to Moses and Aaron and yelled, "What will you do about this? We are starving! My children could die if they don't get more food soon." Others joined him, fueled by the same rage and fear. They even shouted, "If only we had died by the Lord's hand in Egypt!"[6]

The Lord provided meat that very night and a strange kind of bread covered the ground the following morning. Reuben regretted his outburst. With his belly full and his family safe, he recalled the words they sang after God delivered them from slavery; "In your unfailing love you will lead the people you have redeemed."[7] Surely he could trust God's love. Rueben felt a glimmer of contentment.

After three more long months of travel, it was a relief to make camp at the foot of the mountain.[8] Reuben was a bit worried when Moses left to go up the mountain; he wondered if God would be displeased with all of their complaints. When Moses returned and gathered the people, Reuben was humbled to hear God's promise. "Now if you obey me fully and keep my covenant, then out of all nations you will be my treasured possession. Although the whole earth is mine, you

---

5. Exodus 16:3

6. Exodus 16:3, NIV

7. Exodus 15:13, NIV

8. Exodus 19:1

will be for me a kingdom of priests and a holy nation."[9] His heart was full of love for the God who freed him from hopelessness, and Reuben promised obedience.

As awe-inspiring as their escape from Egypt had been, nothing Reuben experienced prepared him for God's presence coming down. Thunder crashed, and lightning crackled in roiling clouds above the mountain. Smoke poured down the sides, and the mountain trembled as the Lord spoke to Moses out of the fire. Moses told them the Lord allowed them to hear God speaking so they would always trust Moses as their leader.[10] Reuben could not imagine doubting God or his chosen leader as he watched Moses ascend the mountain again.

His eager anticipation of what Moses would say when he returned was gradually replaced by impatience and irritation. What was taking so long? Their tedious routine left a lot of time for speculation. Had something happened to Moses? Others began whispering their doubts.

Reuben was restless and increasingly concerned. What was going to happen to them if Moses didn't return? Would God remove the provision of meat and bread? Would they die in this unforgiving desert? Once again, Reuben began crafting plans to provide for his family. He wanted to be prepared for the worst.

Despite his plans—or was it because of them?—Reuben couldn't shake his fears. They grew like a noxious weed, choking out his faith. He wanted to cling to joyous freedom and confident faith, but panic crushed his chest and cut off his breath. Reuben was terrified he wouldn't be able to care for his family. The innocent look in his children's eyes stoked his fears. Tears of frustration over his powerlessness threatened to spill over once again; he couldn't allow them to see his weakness. Reuben vowed to do something; the shame of failing his family was intolerable.

Reuben felt like a soldier preparing for battle. Armed with anger and disdain, he approached a few other heads of families, urging them to join him in confronting Aaron about Moses' absence. Reuben saw how his resolve rippled through the group, shifting the mood from dejection to determination. With a heady sense of control, they surrounded Aaron and demanded a solution. "Come, make us gods

---

9. Exodus 19:5-6, NIV

10. Exodus 19:9

who will go before us. As for this fellow Moses who brought us up out of Egypt, we don't know what has happened to him."[11]

Aaron complied, making an idol, a golden calf representing strength, leadership, and fertility.[12] Reuben felt both empowered and relieved. Turning away from the part of him who promised to obey the Lord, he resolved to remain armored by his anger so he would never feel shame and weakness again.

Veering from Faith to Fear

When the Israelites left Egypt, they escaped the oppression of their hateful masters,[13] but they carried the legacy of years of bondage. God told Moses, "I have indeed seen the misery of my people in Egypt. I have heard them crying out because of their slave drivers, and I am concerned about their suffering."[14] God saw the depth of their pain and rescued them from it, promising to lead them to "a good and spacious land."[15] It is tempting to think the Israelites would never doubt God again. But their deliverance did not miraculously heal the trauma of enslavement; they did not gratefully follow Moses, trusting God despite the trials in the desert. Instead, the narrative is a rollercoaster, with gratitude quickly shifting to heart-pounding fear of the unknown.

Can you relate to the Israelites? They seem so *real.* Praise evaporates like fog dispelled by the heat of fear. Powerlessness and despair overwhelm trust. Anger fuels strategies to control uncertainty. While biblical scholars debate the historical details in Exodus, and the ancient story with its plagues, parted sea, and manna might seem rather bizarre, I connect with these people whose challenges overwhelm their faith. I understand why they could experience a dramatic rescue by a powerful and compassionate God, yet quickly lose trust when starving or feeling abandoned.

---

11. Exodus 32:1, NIV

12. The New Interpreter's Study Bible, NRSV, note for 32:1-6, pg. 131

13. Exodus 1:11-14, NIV

14. Exodus 3:7, NIV

15. Exodus 3:8, NIV

Their bodies still held vulnerable stories from their life in Egypt. We see the impact of unresolved trauma in how they respond to challenges. Experiencing scarcity and uncertainty would have triggered memories of deprivation and powerlessness, shifting them from a Self-led state of safety and connection, to parts-driven mobilization. They could not maintain a broad perspective, recalling God's compassion and promises; threats narrowed their focus to immediate circumstances.

When Fear Takes Over

When fear swamps our internal system, protective members of our inner family step to the forefront. Adverse experiences force parts of us into protective roles. As we've discussed, adversity ranges from trauma to common types of distress. Everyone encounters adversity, so everyone has *exiles*—parts carrying burdens which threaten well-being. When our protectors sense a threat, their reaction is often disproportionate to the immediate danger, because they focus more on the past than the present. Because we all have exiles, we all have protectors—parts forced to adopt various strategies to cope with threats.

The efforts of our dedicated protectors reflect our God-given ability to adapt to threats. No matter the strategy a protector employs, it is *adaptive.* It helps us survive. And their reactions are often "generated by the autonomic nervous system well below the level of conscious awareness. This is not the brain making a cognitive choice."[16] The energy of sympathetic arousal—our "fight or flight" response to a threat—fuels protectors. If they don't successfully dispel the threat, others disconnect us, shifting us to parasympathetic shut-down.

Our protective strategies are impressively adaptive but are not thoughtful, Self-led responses. That is why the actions our protectors take sometimes seem at odds with the values and beliefs we would say we have when we are centered and grounded—when we feel safe.

Protectors hijack the leadership of the inner family—usurping the role Self is designed to play. You might have heard protectors called the "false self," a term I've encountered in spiritual literature. While it is accurate to say our protectors do not reflect our most authentic selves, referring to them as false feels critical and

16. *The Polyvagal Theory in Therapy: Engaging the Rhythm of Regulation,* Deb Dana, pg. 6

can impede the desire to develop a relationship with them. Seen through the eyes of the Self, protectors are valued members of the inner family.

Protectors are well-intentioned, dedicated, hard-working members of the internal family who believe their job is imperative. Their jobs are not their essence—it is not *who* they are; it is what they *do* to protect you. When a threat is resolved—when exiles can tell their stories and release their burdens—protectors give up these jobs and return to playing their preferred roles in the inner family. As you learn about different types of protectors, you will catch glimpses of their inate qualities twisted into adaptive strategies due to adversity.

When we turn our attention inside, protectors are typically the first members of the inner family we encounter. We aim to build relationships with them, not cast them out of the family! Identifying common protective strategies helps build awareness of their presence, the first step in cultivating relationships.

Introducing Your Risk Managers

One category of protectors scans the environment for potential threats, attempting to intervene to avoid disaster *proactively*. They are all about controlling everything possible to minimize the chance that the pain your exiles hold floods your system. Think of them as "risk managers."

All protectors are fear-driven; they fear something will trigger an exile, and you will be overwhelmed by the exile's pain—intense emotions, distorted beliefs, and distressing images. Our proactive "risk managers" use various strategies to avoid this risk—including analyzing and rationalizing, hypervigilance, minimizing/bypassing/denial, criticizing/shaming, perfectionism, and caregiving/overfunctioning. They play the comparison game where losing is unacceptable. After introducing them, I will walk you through exercises to help you build relationships with your hard-working risk managers.

Rationalizing and Analyzing

In Western culture, *rationalizing or analyzing* is one of our dominant protective strategies. We quickly pivot from feeling emotions to thinking about them. Our protectors like to be in control, and one way to manage emotions is to attempt to make sense of them. Rationalizing happens when we feel emotional about our circumstances or learn of someone else's struggle. We will notice this part of ourselves saying something like, "This reaction makes no sense" or "I shouldn't be upset; it won't help solve the problem."

These protectors disconnect us from the sensations in our bodies—from vital emotional information we need to function optimally. Ironically, when we are cut off from our emotions, neuroscience shows we lose our ability to reason well.[17]

Our internal "analysts" also disconnect us from one another. Rather than empathically feeling with someone in distress, they put up a wall of logic that shields us. "If they followed the rules, they wouldn't be in this situation." Can you feel how statements like this distance you from the discomfort of unpleasant emotions?

Similarly, our thinkers also distance us from our exiles. The more our thinkers and analysts dominate our internal family, the more difficult it is to connect with the wounded parts they are protecting. Thinking about what happened is not a substitute for connecting directly with the part of us who holds pain so they can share their story.

These energetic "thinkers" introduce us to the paradox of protectors. Their gifts are vital, and yet sometimes, an impediment to ideal functioning. Protectors are members of the internal family who initially contributed essential qualities like critical thinking. Reasoning is vital for life. One of the crucial developmental tasks is to learn emotional regulation from our caregivers, so we can benefit from a combination of emotion and reason as we navigate life. But when adversity thrusts one of these thinking parts into overdrive to protect the inner system, their energy blocks access to healing resources. These parts, who deploy logic as a strategy to cut off feelings they fear, reduce our ability to use an ideal combination of emotion *plus* thoughtful reason.

Often, clients are surprised when they learn about their inner analysts. They say, "I thought that was just me!" We are culturally conditioned, especially in the West, to value reason over emotion, and these parts of us earn praise. As we develop relationships with them, they can return to contributing valuable qualities rather than dominating the internal family.

---

17. Antonio Damasio, *Descartes' Error*, pg. xvi

Hypervigilance

Hypervigilant protectors are like sentries posted at the entrance to the castle. They are armed and armored, ready to fight to eliminate a threat. Constantly scanning the environment, they evaluate safety and act independently of the Self or even other members of the inner family who have different ideas of how to respond to circumstances. They are likely to imagine worst-case scenarios as a means of being prepared for any eventuality.

Imagine being blindsided by some kind of attack—either physical or emotional. You were unguarded and unprepared, and the force of the blow—literally or metaphorically—knocked you down. Your world no longer felt safe because the attack came out of nowhere, leaving you battered and raw. Protectors never want this to happen to you again, and one way to avoid it is by being hypervigilant.

I imagine the Israelites having hypervigilant protectors because of their history of enslavement in Egypt. Powerlessness and despair—intense emotions inevitable in their context—provoked protectors who reacted every time the Israelites encountered challenges in the desert. They wanted to regain control; a barrage of unknowns activated past experiences of helplessness. These alert protectors lack the perspective of Self; they are laser-focused on risk. They do not think, "God rescued us and provided beyond our imagining, so we can continue to trust God." Instead, they see uncertainty and take matters into their own hands.

Hypervigilant protectors are particularly prominent when your story contains trauma. Traumatic events involve powerlessness. Powerlessness is one of our most vulnerable states, and it feels like an intolerable risk to your inner system. To shield you from vulnerability, part of you adopts the role of hypervigilant manager, vowing "never again." They constantly assess threats and craft "what-if" narratives to avoid further attacks. Your body's natural ability to mobilize in the face of risk and to relax after the crisis passes shifts to a constant state of readiness. These dedicated sentries might block authentic and intimate relationships because they have difficulty trusting others.

Can you see how adaptive this is, how essential they were to your survival? It might be surprising to feel your heart opening to a sentry who is always on duty. They consume a lot of energy, which can be frustrating and exhausting. Interestingly, when you connect with them and ask them what they would rather do if they didn't have to protect you in this way, they frequently say they want to rest. They are exhausted, but their dedication to your safety takes precedence over their preferences. If you sense you have a hypervigilant protector, see if you can feel a measure of gratitude for their efforts. Notice anything else that accompanies that feeling.

Minimizing, Bypassing, and Denial

Another group of risk managers *minimize, bypass,* or *deny* the impact of challenges to avoid vulnerability. They represent the interplay of personal experience and cultural conditioning.

In America, we celebrate stoicism as strength in the face of trials. The message about suffering is often, "Get over it." Whether you are dealing with physical or mental illness, relationship difficulties, the death of a loved one, financial challenges, or any of the myriad issues that derail our lives, you feel pressure to act as if it's "no big deal." Proactive risk managers are attuned to cultural norms—such as the urgency of "getting over" pain—so they use minimizing, bypassing, and denial to make us comply. They go along to get along. They do not want to risk being an outsider or having you appear "weak."

Our churches are full of protectors who are experts in minimizing, bypassing, and denying suffering. Bible verses are plucked out of context and slapped on situations to avoid vulnerability. As with any protective strategy, they are well-intentioned despite the impact of these hurtful reactions. Suffering presents a thorny theological challenge for people who believe God loves us and "in all things...works for the good of those who love him."[18] Despite being rescued from enslavement, the Israelites struggled to maintain faith when they feared for their survival or were terrified their leader had abandoned them. God's goodness is not necessarily apparent when tragedy strikes, or people are oppressed. And that's scary.

We can have faith in God's goodness. God "is love," and Love is *for* you. You are beloved, no matter your circumstances or story. Your pain is like a beacon that draws God's mercy. God is present with you when you experience hard—or even devastating—things. "Even though I walk through the darkest valley, I will fear

---

18. Romans 8:28, NIV

no evil, for you are with me."[19] The psalmist does not deny or bypass the presence of evil in countless forms of suffering. Rather than the counterfeit comfort these protective strategies offer, our true comfort comes from knowing we are not alone. God is with us, and that's what it means for God to work "for the good of those who love him."

The good news is that doubting God's goodness—when God seems absent and your circumstances seem hopeless—is not sinful. A prominent biblical scholar, Peter Enns, says, "The opposite of faith is not doubt. The opposite of faith is a rigorous certainty...Doubt is the engine that makes faith go."[20] It is normal, natural, and entirely human to doubt God's goodness in the face of uncertainty, trials, and tragedy. We are invited to work out our faith in fear and trembling,[21] not in forced bravado. God can handle your doubt; God does not judge it. Jesus says, "Come to me, all you who are weary and burdened...and you will find rest for your souls.[22]

It is not easy to sit with the tension between tragedy and trust. The mystery of why a loving God allows suffering provokes protectors who are allergic to vulnerability. One way they steer clear of uncertainty is through spiritual bypassing. When someone is in the midst of a trial, and we reflexively tell them, "Remember! God works for the good of those who love him!" a protector has taken over. Other statements our protectors use to shield us from vulnerability—such as "God won't give you more than you can handle," "They are in a better place," or "This too shall pass"—shut the door on connection, leaving others isolated in their pain.

When we are Self-and Spirit-led, we come alongside others without minimizing their pain, offering a spiritual bypass, or denying the difficulty of maintaining faith in a loving God amid trials. We all need the gentle presence of loving connection, so it is crucial to recognize the work of these protectors. When we catch ourselves minimizing, bypassing, or denying pain, we will know they are on the job, doing

---

19. Psalm 23:4, NIV

20. GMA interview March 17, 2023 https://www.goodmorningamerica.com/gma3/video/faith-friday-lifes-curveballs-bring-us-closer-god-97943889

21. Philippians 2:12, NIV

22. Matthew 11:28-30, NIV

their best to protect us from vulnerability. You can move from awareness to connection by letting them know you appreciate how they are trying to help you.

Criticizing and Shaming

Your risk managers also *criticize or shame* to control you and others they see as a threat. These protectors proactively criticize or shame you to avoid a mistake that provokes external sources of criticism or shame. They can be nasty bullies who nitpick your appearance, communication, and how you move your body. Work—inside and outside the home—is also a favorite target. Did you do something "right," well enough, or timely? Insults such as, "You idiot! How could you let that happen?" reflect their presence. They latch onto others' comments and repeat them, lest you forget you fell short.

Typically, they adopted their strategy when you were relatively young. Children receive input from parents and other adults constantly; it is how they learn and develop. But, inevitably, some of that input is harsh—or perceived as harsh. When an authority figure is routinely critical, particularly one who is a source of security, a child internalizes the message, "I'm bad" or "I'm not good enough." Shame accompanies these distorted beliefs, so your internal family adapts by exiling the burdened little one and adopting protective strategies to avoid further criticism and shame. The more severe or unrelenting the external criticism, the more powerful and unrelenting your protectors will be in attempting to control you to avoid it.

Understandably, inner critics and shamers are unpopular. Other members of your inner family and external "authorities" attempt to stifle them. Even among people unfamiliar with the idea of multiplicity you will hear the term "inner critic." Typically, others urge you to control or silence them.

If you have ever tried to shame your inner shamer, you know how futile this is. They do not think it is safe to stop trying to control you. They have one eye on the past—when someone shamed you —and the other eye on the outside world that is, for them, replete with threats. If the part of you who dislikes them tries to control them, they intensify their efforts.

Our practice is to befriend these dedicated protectors. They do their job under what is often withering criticism from others! They are so committed to your safety that they accept they're hated and do their job anyway. When you turn toward them with curiosity, asking them to share about how they are trying to help you and why, they will be surprised. They may never have been greeted with anything other than disdain. Often, you will have to negotiate with other members of the inner family who dislike or fear them so you can have a one-to-one conversation. But when you do, they will show you the chapters in your story where shame provoked their strategy. Your heart will soften, and you will feel compassion for their heroic efforts.

Perfectionism

One of the most potent protectors uses *perfectionism* to avoid risks. Protectors who use perfectionism in an attempt to control are similar to those who criticize and shame. (It's not unusual for our inner family members to align with other parts who have similar fears and strategies.) Your inner perfectionist also wants to avoid the shame of falling short—of missing some external standard. Any perceived mistake represents an unacceptable risk.

A perfectionistic protector is rigid; there is no flexibility when they are in charge. You can feel the difference between their energy and the desire to strive for excellence. One is rigid, and the other is an intention you choose.

For perfectionistic protectors, it is not acceptable to be or look "good enough." Anything representing you to the world—appearance, home, work, opinions, needs, behaviors—is subject to their microscopic review. Often, they focus on your body and any perceived deficiencies because of cultural messages that idealize certain body types and conflate image and worth.

Perfectionist parts spend significant energy checking and rechecking your image, work product, and relationship dynamics. "Did I say the right thing?" "What did that expression mean? Does this outfit make me look bad?" "I can't let them drop by! My house isn't perfectly in order." "What did that colleague mean by, 'That will do.'? I failed. I need to work harder." They are focused on anything others interpret as a mistake—let alone failure.

They are never satisfied that you are immune from attack, so they prevent you from trying new things—from being a beginner. Thoughts such as, "If I can't do it right, I shouldn't do it at all," stop you before you risk not knowing how to do something "perfectly." Their message: There is one right way to do or to be. The dilemma is that perfection is elusive because, no matter how you present yourself, you feel pressure from your perfectionist to do better.

In their eyes, mistakes don't make you human; they make you worthless. They believe any evidence that you are less-than-perfect will risk unacceptable—or unsurvivable—criticism, leading to shame.

These protectors consume significant energy. When they are in charge, it's difficult to have sufficient energy left over for living your life, let alone feeling joy or freedom. The amount of energy they use to protect you reflects their concern about vulnerability. They fear if they relax, someone will judge you, and you will be deemed deficient. Recognizing that their intensity is rooted in fear—perhaps even terror—opens space for compassion. When you feel compassion for them, you can extend it to them, creating a space for connection. Being with them as compassion flows from your heart to theirs builds their awareness of your resources. Ultimately, consistent connection allows them to trust your leadership.

Caregiving and Overfunctioning

On the opposite end of the spectrum from your critical, shaming, and perfectionistic protectors, you will find *caregivers* and *overfunctioners.* These risk managers do everything they can for others without regard for your needs. They are your boundary violators, doing things others can and should do for themselves. This differs from an adult's care for a young child or an elder who cannot care for themselves. It is caregiving rooted in anxiety—the fear that you will be abandoned or neglected if you do not care for others.

If "overfunctioning" is a new term, consider these protectors as "people-pleasers." They will do whatever it takes to ensure everyone else is happy without regard to what makes *you* happy. Your needs are either secondary or of no concern.

Often, they adopted this strategy during childhood when adults were not functioning fully because of mental illness, addiction, or other stressors. Caregivers who were supposed to be a source of security were distant or disconnected because of their concerns. Survival is at stake when caregivers aren't attentive to a child's needs. The resulting anxiety fuels caregiving and overfunctioning protectors who take on responsibilities that belong to adults.

They work tirelessly, believing their strategy will build the bonds that keep you safe.

As with other protectors, caregivers and overfunctioners can be motivated by cultural norms, working to ensure the safety of belonging. Patriarchy has been a powerful force in shaping our internal families. It has spawned dedicated caretakers and overfunctioners because women internalized the connection between these behaviors and their worth. I also think of men like Reuben, who felt weak and shameful if they couldn't provide for their families. The message of patriarchy doesn't make room for sharing this responsibility or for seasons throughout a relationship when one partner is the primary provider, circumstances change, and the other takes the lead. Shared responsibilities for both caregiving and provision support flexible responses to changing conditions, benefitting both partners. Flexibility is a mark of health; rigidity signals that protectors need attention.

Overfunctioning is pervasive among women. When caregiving roles are one's primary identity, it is difficult to accept help. If our overfunctioning protectors gave up their jobs, who would we—and they—be? Support from others feels threatening to this identity, so we don't try to reason with protectors to convince them to give up their role. Fear—not logic—motivates their efforts. Building relationships with them develops sufficient trust in the Self to allow us into the tender stories fueling their actions.

While overfunctioning is common among women generally, it is especially pervasive in many church communities. I attended a seminary for my master's degree in marriage and family therapy, and many of my clients identify as Christians. I have seen how messages from the Church about serving others and denying ourselves energize overfunctioning, caregiving protectors. Even the Great Commandment is often misquoted as "loving God and others" without reference to loving ourselves. If the church is a source of authority and security, and the message—whether overt or covert—is that women in particular should prioritize others' needs over their own, these protectors are listening. Updating them with a more expansive and nuanced view about balancing our and others' needs can help them relax and trust your leadership.

Each of the risk managers we surveyed in this chapter attempts to avoid threats *proactively*. This is not an exhaustive list; parts are creative in adopting various approaches. But they all scan the environment, hoping to avoid being blindsided, shamed, or neglected. These protectors will use whatever tactic is available to control you so the burdens held by exiles don't overwhelm the system. Your needs are not their concern; their job is to keep you safe. They are tireless and dedicated members of your internal family who believe their role is vital in avoiding what they most fear: that your system will be overwhelmed when an exile is triggered. Often, they are such dominant parts of your system you might be surprised to learn they are not your whole self!

It's easy to scorn the Israelites for their desperate attempt to restore certainty in the face of unbearable mystery. How could they believe a golden calf—a forbidden idol—was superior to the God who delivered them and miraculously provided for them in the desert? But when we understand the peril posed by shame, powerlessness, despair, and terror, judgment fades and empathy grows. We recognize how our protectors opt for control over uncertainty and how their limited perspective constrains trust.

But what happens when proactive protection strategies fail? That's what we will look at in the next chapter.

Spiritual Practice: Connecting with Protectors Who Manage Risk

Establishing relationships with your hard-working protectors is a transformative practice. It facilitates a shift from a system where parts independently do their jobs without regard for you as the leader, to a more flexible and harmonious team working together toward a goal.

Building relationships with key protectors is an opportunity to introduce yourself, allowing them to experience the value of having access to God-given resources such as creativity, clarity, and calm, and then go forward with arms linked, working together.

Author Shannon K. Evans says, "We are changed only by deeply listening to ourselves, then accepting—*believing*—what we hear."[23] Each member of your inner family has a story to share. For protectors, the story is about their mission—the strategy adopted to help you navigate the impact of adversity. As you extend the grace of accepting them just as they are, of believing their story, you are moving toward wholeness.

Perhaps you already identified a protector you'd like to get to know. Recall a recent experience that activated them—when you felt their presence. If you're unsure where to start, remember a recent incident where you were critical of yourself or others, violating boundaries by doing more for someone than was yours to do, feeling anxious, or replaying an incident repeatedly.

As you notice thoughts, emotions, and sensations, turn your attention inside. The goal is to develop a Self-to-part relationship using the following steps. I will suggest natural breaks so you can do bits and pieces until you are ready to work through the whole process. I encourage you to jot notes about your interactions in your journal.

Awareness of a Protector

- Notice your inner experience, including sensations, thoughts, emotions, and images.
- If you feel overwhelmed, breathe deeply, and exhale slowly. Imagine your breath creating a healing space for connection.
- What feels most intense? Bring your attention to it.
- You've just identified a member of your internal family!
    - Where are they located in your body?
    - What emotions do they hold?
    - Do you see them?

---

23. Shannon K. Evans newsletter 8/5/23

- You can pause here and make a note in your journal about this valuable member of your internal family.

Unblending—Differentiating Between the Self and the Protector

- Return to the protector you identified. You are ready to continue connecting with them when you sense their presence (through their emotions, thoughts, or sensations).
- Ask yourself, "***How am I feeling toward this part of me?***"
    - We ask this because there are many members of your internal family, but you can only connect with one at a time. I use the metaphor of a director working with actors on a stage. You want to shine the spotlight on one member of the cast of characters while others wait in the wings for their turn.
    - In response to the question, "How am I feeling toward it?" you might hear, "I'm afraid of it," "I don't like it," or "I'm annoyed by it." Or, your heart is racing, your breath is shallow, or there's an impulse to run.
    - Anything *other than* one of the 8 Cs (or some other manifestation of love) means that other parts are present. This is often the case! We are multiple, after all. Acknowledge whoever is there, and let them know you value their input but can only connect with one part at a time. Then ask them to give you space and tell them you want to connect with them when it's their turn.
- Now, notice how you are feeling toward the original part. Are you at least somewhat curious and open to connecting? You do not have to be 100% Self-led to connect with a member of your internal family. We assess for sufficient Self-energy to know that enough love is present to create a safe and trusting bond.
- Note your response to this part of you in your journal. Which "C" quality does it inspire? How does it feel to realize their activity is not

your whole identity? What happens in your inner system as you imagine befriending them and working together, rather than them toiling alone or being criticized by other parts of you?

Befriending A Protector

- The next step, and the heart of this practice, is ***befriending***. While the idea of connecting with a part of you might feel strange, you connect with people all the time. You know how to relate to others! This is no different. When Self leads, your creativity and curiosity will guide you as you connect with a member of your inner family.
- Some helpful questions to get you started:
    - How are you trying to help me? What is your job?
    - Do you like your job?
    - How long have you been doing it?
    - What do you need from me?
- As you learn more about their strategy, maintain awareness of your feelings toward the protector. Other parts may pop back in with commentary or attitudes that block the flow of curiosity. If that happens, ask them to wait their turn.
- This is a relationship, not an interrogation, so notice the response to your questions. Some parts aren't very verbal. Their response could be a shift in sensations or emotions. You will be able to tell whether they are open to connecting with you or whether they are reluctant.
- If the part of you is not responsive or is snarky, remember they might have been toiling on behalf of the inner system for years without any recognition or assistance—or despite others criticizing them for what they do. Let them know you appreciate their efforts!
- You can also ask questions to assess how they view you:

    - Do you trust I am here to help you?

    - What would help you trust me more?

- Whenever the current conversation is complete, thank them for being willing to connect. Let them know you would like to continue the conversation another time.

- Jot some notes in your journal about how it felt to get to know this prominent member of your inner family. How did they initially respond? What happened as you remained connected and curious? How do you feel about committing to an ongoing relationship? What emotions arise as you think of this new acquaintance?

- If parts of you feel silly, skeptical, or reluctant about talking to "parts," that is understandable! It helps to remember their responses are rooted in fear. It's unsettling to the system to do something different. While, ultimately, all members of the internal family want or need your attention, it is a change, and change provokes a variety of responses. Practice being with whatever arises, allowing it to be just as it is. As you extend this gracious presence to your inner system, they will relax and trust you more.

Deepening the Relationship

Befriending parts of you takes time and intention. When you think of this process as developing a relationship with a part of you who works diligently to protect you, it will feel like an opportunity rather than a task.

- When you return to a protector, you should again ask, "How am I feeling toward them?"

    - It is helpful to note other parts who are present. Often, the same ones will show up. For example, if you meet with a caretaker, you might also notice a part annoyed with them for doing "too much."

    - Ask the annoyed one to give you space, but let them know you'd like to meet with them later. If you have two friends in the room but only pay attention to one of them, the other will feel slighted. The same guideline applies to internal relationships.

- As you meet with the protector, notice their response. Do you feel you've made a new friend? Do they trust that you have something valuable to offer?

- Spend time getting to know their job, how they feel about it, and extending appreciation for their role.

- Jot notes in your journal about your interactions with each member of your inner family.

Make a "Parts Map"

As you experiment and develop relationships with different members of your internal family, it's not uncommon to be overwhelmed by the many different parts of you or to be confused about whether what you notice is one part or a variety of parts. Remember, you are getting to know members of your internal family, and family members have relationships with one another! They are connected, and they have opinions about one another. A "parts map" helps depict both individual parts and how they relate to other members of the system. We gain clarity by externalizing what is happening inside.

I assure you, no artistic ability is required! You can depict parts with words, colors, shapes, or photos. You can also use objects like stones or toy action figures. You might draw a spiky ball, color it red, and label it with its role.

As you identify individual parts, notice relationships between them. Which ones are in conflict? Which are aligned? How do they relate to Self?

Chapter Seven

When the Pain in the Story is Too Great

Selections from the Gospels

Eli[1] was becoming increasingly concerned about the teacher from Nazareth. Mobs of people who knew nothing of the law were being deceived![2] Apparently, Jesus did not understand how vital purity was for God's people. How could they please God—reclaiming their independence from pagans who surrounded and infiltrated their nation—without strictly observing the Torah?[3] Eli feared God would not restore Israel if Jesus continued to persuade people to violate the law.

Troubled by hearing about miraculous healings on the Sabbath—something Eli felt could not be of God—he went to the synagogue where Jesus would be. His heart began to race when Jesus told a man with a shriveled hand to stand up in front of everyone.[4] Jesus asked, "Which is lawful on the Sabbath: to do good or to do evil, to save life or to kill?" Eli was stunned and insulted.[5] How dare Jesus accuse the religious leaders of being on the side of evil!? They lived to restore God's people, and strict observance of the Torah was their only hope!

---

1. Eli is a fictional Pharisee.

2. John 7:47-52, NIV

3. *The New Testament in its World,* N.T. Wright and Michael F. Bird, pg. 125

4. Mark 3:1-3, NIV

5. Mark 3:5, NIV

When Jesus healed the man, Eli left, along with the other Pharisees, determined to find a way to stop him, even if they had to kill him.[6]

Eli tossed and turned, unable to sleep. He had devoted his life to serving the Lord, learning the law, and guiding others in faithfully adhering to it. Now, a massive crowd from Galilee, as well as people from Judea and Jerusalem, across the Jordan, and around Tyre and Sidon—swarms of people who had heard the reports of healing and came to see for themselves—followed *Jesus*.[7] He felt like the religious leaders were losing control. His gut churned as rage coursed through his body. Why was Jesus able to cast out evil spirits, when they could not? Surely he was in league with the ruler of demons.[8] The leaders must stop him.

A few weeks later, Eli went to the temple and saw Jesus, again, teaching a crowd of people who seemed captivated by him. Eli burned with indignation. How dare he desecrate the temple devoted to maintaining the purity of God's people! Just then a group of his fellow Pharisees brought in a woman caught in adultery and reminded Jesus that the law required stoning.[9] Eli thought, "Finally! A test will reveal this rebel as a fraud." Jesus replied, "Let any one of you who is without sin be the first to throw a stone at her."[10] Stunned, Eli could do nothing but walk away, his throat tight with fear and grief over the increasing influence of this clever manipulator.

Eli had always been able to rely on certainty for security. Now he felt unmoored; his emotions careened from fear to rage to despair. Searching for answers, Eli wondered if Jesus was God's way of testing their commitment to the Torah. If Jesus continued to turn people from God's law, their future as a nation was at risk. Eli felt compelled to act.

Perhaps Eli could persuade Jesus that strict adherence to the law was Israel's salvation. He decided to invite Jesus to his home for a meal, where he and his friends could rebuke Jesus. After they sat down, and before he could reprimand

---

6. Mark 3:6

7. Mark 3:7-8

8. Matthew 12:24, NRSV

9. John 8:2-6, NIV

10. John 8:8, NIV

Jesus for failing to wash before eating, Jesus said, "Now you Pharisees clean the outside of the cup and of the dish, but inside you are full of greed and wickedness."[11] Eli felt his face flush with anger. The audacity of this man, coming into his home and insulting him! Eli was further shocked to sense a part of him who wanted to physically attack Jesus, then and there.

Before Eli could respond, Jesus escalated his critique. "Woe to you Pharisees, because you give God a tenth of your mint, rue, and all other kinds of garden herbs, but you neglect justice and the love of God."[12] Eli sat in stunned silence as Jesus accused good men dedicated to the Lord of loading people down with burdens when they followed the Torah.[13] How dare he mock their faithfulness!

As Jesus pelted him with accusations, Eli's heart raced, and every muscle in his body tensed for a fight. He frantically searched for ways to refute the allegations as words like arrows tipped with poison penetrated his soul: blind guides, vipers, murderers, hypocrites.[14]

"Enough! Get out of my house!" Eli's rage was consuming, and although he longed to eliminate this threat to God's people, he knew he couldn't act alone.

Eli slumped into a chair as adrenaline ebbed, leaving him unsteady. He thought Romans were their worst enemies. It was heartbreaking and terrifying for one of their own to challenge God's chosen leaders. Eli remembered seeing Jesus as a boy in the temple courts; he showed such promise![15] Grief and fear warred within Eli as he wondered how they would deal with this threat to their nation.

Eli spent many hours over the next few months deep in prayer and thought, troubled by the continued influence of the so-called teacher. One day, he headed for the temple, hoping to settle his nerves with soothing rituals. Before he saw the temple grounds, he heard shouting. What was going on?

The sight that greeted Eli made his blood run cold; he felt goosebumps all over his body. Jesus had thrown out everyone buying or selling animals required

---

11. Luke 11:39, NRSV

12. Luke 11:42, NIV

13. Luke 11:46, NIV

14. Matthew 23:13-39

15. Luke 2:46-48

for sacrifices and the money changers on whom they relied. He had overturned tables, and merchants were scurrying away like thieves about to be arrested. The arrogance of this man! Didn't he know sacrifices were an essential act of worship? To make matters worse, Jesus healed the blind and lame, and children were singing his praises![16]

Jesus threatened everything Eli understood about living as God's people under the security of the law. If they let him go on like this, everyone would believe in him, and the Romans would come and take away the temple and the nation.[17] The chief priests and elders shared his concerns. They met and devised a plan to arrest and kill Jesus. Eli was confident God would be with them, empowering them in extinguishing this intolerable threat.

Context Influences Our Conduct

How could Israel's religious leaders collude with their foes—the despised Roman authorities—to kill Jesus, one of their own? Didn't they feel the love that motivated Jesus' ministry? Couldn't they see how Jesus embodied the Lord's desire for Israel to "act justly...love mercy...and walk humbly" with their God?[18] Why did healings provoke legalism instead of praise? Cultural context helps us understand their response to Jesus—and gain insight into some of *our* protective reactions as well.

New Testament scholar N.T. Wright provides vital historical context for Jesus' conflict with religious leaders. Jesus' contemporaries—Jewish, Greek, and Roman—used honor and shame "as a way of enforcing their particular values, and urging conformity to a particular ethos."[19] Honor affirmed a person's value, and shame eroded it. When Jesus challenged religious authorities—and crowds credited him with greater wisdom and power—in the language of his day he was

---

16. Matthew 21:12-15

17. John 11:48, paraphrase of NIV

18. Micah 6:8, NIV

19. *The New Testament in its World: An Introduction to the History, Literature, and Theology of the First Christians,* N.T. Wright and Michael F. Bird, pg 114

increasing his honor and shaming his opponents.[20] Killing Jesus was a reaction to the shame of dishonor.[21] Then and now, cultural norms and values are powerful forces that shape our internal family. And shame remains one of the most significant risks to well-being.

Pharisees derived honor from strict adherence to Torah. They believed God would honor their faithfulness by restoring Israel to independence from Roman rule. Pharisees were the group "filled with intense fervor to win the hearts and minds of the people to their program, and merciless towards those whom they saw as subverting the national customs."[22] Their focus on purity protected the Jewish identity and the hope of liberation.[23] They were well-intentioned, believing strict adherence to the Law would liberate God's people. Jesus clashed with the Pharisees "because his kingdom-agenda for Israel demanded that Israel leave off its frantic search for national purity...and embrace instead the proper vocation to be the light of the world."[24]

At every turn, Jesus challenged the religious leaders—which they interpreted as an attack on their honor and a source of shame. He threatened the security they derived from their interpretation of the law. Religious leaders plotted to kill Jesus because he represented an existential threat.

Protectors Do What it Takes to Eliminate Threats

All of the protective members of our internal family are motivated by fear, and their greatest fear is that we will be overwhelmed by unbearable emotions. When our risk-managing protectors try and fail to contain pain, a second category of protectors rushes in to deal with it. Dr. Schwartz named them "firefighters"

20. Ibid, pg. 114

21. Ibid, pg. 115

22. Ibid, pg. 125

23. Ibid, pg. 126

24. Ibid, pg. 128

because they are like first responders—they do whatever it takes to numb the pain and restore a sense of safety.[25]

Think of how firefighters arrive at the scene of a fire, kick down doors and turn on hoses to douse flames without concern for the damage it will cause. They don't care about furniture; the house is on fire! Our inner firefighters have a "do whatever it takes, no matter the cost" attitude. Just as religious leaders rationalized plotting to kill Jesus because his ministry threatened their worldview, protectors can react in extreme ways to contain threats.

When strategies used by *proactive* risk managers fail to contain exiles' burdens—painful emotions and sensations, distorted beliefs, and distressing images—*reactive* firefighters jump in. They attempt to numb the emotional firestorm caused by exiles. As long as "it works quickly and is effective," firefighters use whatever is available to soothe or distract us from emotional pain.[26]

Firefighters don't immediately use the most radical approach to contain the threat. We typically have a hierarchy of firefighter activities that escalate in intensity until the threat is resolved.[27] The ladder of strategies typically looks something like work/exercise/entertainment/spirituality, food/sex, rage, dissociation, addiction/compulsive behaviors, and self-harm/suicidal ideation/suicide. Because this chapter addresses some difficult and potentially activating material, please be aware of its impact on your system. Practice kindness if your body says this is not the time to read it. It will be here when you're ready.

Work, Exercise, Entertainment, and Spirituality

Routine activities such as work, exercise, entertainment, and spirituality are essential to our lives. Purposeful work, moving our bodies, enjoying various playful and creative activities, and engaging in spiritual practices all contribute to well-being. However, firefighters can also use each of these to distract us from distress.

---

25. *Internal Family Systems Therapy (2nd. ed.),* Richard C. Schwartz and Martha Sweezy, pg. 35

26. Ibid, pg. 105

27. Ibid, pg. 35

If loneliness or boredom marks the end of the workday, a firefighter might remind you of your task list so you return to work. When you think of leaving the office, that part of you reminds you of another task, and hours slip by before you finally head home. If there's chaos or conflict in your home—challenges that can stir up feelings of inadequacy, anxiety, or overwhelm—parts can use work to distract you. And, if your proactive protectors fail to avoid criticism from a supervisor or colleague, reactive protectors can take over and become taskmasters who will not allow downtime. And culturally, workaholism is North America's most socially accepted addiction.

Exercise can also be used to numb painful emotions. If your reflection in the mirror provokes criticism or shame, part of you can keep you in the gym much longer than you planned. The relentless barrage of messages about "ideal" bodies also stirs up protectors who can take over and push you to the point of injury. Anxiety can also trigger parts to use exercise to excess because the calming effect of endorphins eases the discomfort of anxiety. While moderate exercise is essential for most people, if a part of you will not allow days off for rest and recovery, it is likely using exercise to manage internal discomfort.

Your favorite streaming or social media app provides a much-needed break from productivity. And, they can be a black hole sucking you in for hours if part of you is afraid that stopping will allow space for distressing emotions. There's a cost when a firefighter uses entertainment to distract you. Work doesn't get done, you don't get the rest you need, and if your go-to is social media, you might be exposed to content that *intensifies* anxiety and depression.

Ideally, spiritual practices strengthen our connection with God, one of the most significant sources of comfort when we are suffering. However, suppose something uncomfortable like grief surfaces, and we reflexively recite a verse or hymn containing a message that minimizes or even rebukes our feelings. Spiritual bypassing is another strategy that protectors use to distance us from distress.

When the threat is not severe, firefighters will use activities you are already engaged in to tamp out flames before they become a blaze. It is a clever way to distract us from unpleasant feelings—a necessary adaptation to the impact of adverse experiences. However, our goal is for the Self to lead the inner family. When we notice a firefighter routinely using one of these activities to excess or to avoid unpleasantness, our practice is to turn toward them to learn why they are so active. What is the problem they are trying to solve?

Food and Sex

Nourishing ourselves with food is an essential source of pleasure and connection with others. Similarly, sexual activity is an integral part of relationship intimacy. God created us to enjoy both food and sex, yet these are two areas where the complex array of instinctual, cultural, and—particularly in the case of sex—religious influences impact how these needs play out in our lives. Add that your firefighters can use these activities to protect you from pain, and you have a complex knot to untangle.

Families—which represent a variety of ethnicities and histories—have practices and rules that have a profound influence on our attitudes and behaviors concerning food. For example, some groups use food as a go-to source of comfort when conflict erupts. We can see how the threat of disunion in a family would give rise to inviting everyone to a common table to restore bonds. In other cases, when ancestors fled famine, an abundance of food is reassuring. This highlights the underlying benefit of many of our protective strategies. Often, they are a positive approach that becomes extreme when protectors fear we will be overwhelmed by pain.

Family habits can become a challenge when an individual's only tool for distress is to soothe or control with food. In some cases, there's a complicating element of rules about complying with cultural norms about bodies. Family members can shame both men and women for weight gain or weight loss.

If rules about eating are severe—never being allowed to eat "forbidden" foods—children do not learn to manage their natural cravings (for things like sugar), they simply learn to hide them. They might keep a stash of sweets in their room, gobbling them up out of fear of being caught. Rigid rules can lead to a pattern of bingeing and purging in a desperate cycle of overeating and attempting to comply with expectations about weight.

Your protectors listen carefully to family rules and cultural norms. Risk managers want you to comply and conform to avoid threats, and when their strategies—such as criticizing you for indulging in dessert—fail to contain pain, your firefighters can use food to numb it. Or, if one of your exiles is triggered, you might reach for a bag of chips or a quart of ice cream and eat far more than you usually would. One client noticed that she drank a lot of coffee despite knowing it would affect her sleep. As we explored the days when that occurred, she realized it was a reaction to feeling depressed. She had a firefighter who used caffeine to shift her mood and restore a sense of safety.

Sadly, in some cases, children do not have access to sufficient nutrition. This can, understandably, lead protectors to provoke over-eating, even many years later, when the situation may have changed.

As complex and multilayered as attitudes about food are, sex is often even more complicated. Everyone navigates a labyrinth of rules and regulations from various "authorities" concerning one of our most intense and intimate experiences as humans. The emotional impact of narratives about sex, sexual orientation, and specific sexual experiences presents complex challenges for our internal family members. They can burden our system with painful emotions such as shame or loneliness and beliefs that we are unworthy or unlovable. These burdens are a threat to the system, giving rise to a variety of protective strategies.

Sometimes sex becomes a tool protectors use to numb or distract. Because of the intense feelings it arouses and the biochemical release of so-called happy hormones[28] —oxytocin and dopamine—it makes sense that firefighters would use sex to douse the flames of torment erupting from exiles. Compulsive masturbation, pornography, and impulsive sexual encounters provide a respite from distress. Promiscuous or risky behavior—often shamed by internal and external critics—can be a strategy to avoid loneliness and low self-worth. Ironically—and sometimes tragically—cultural attitudes such as purity culture distort sexual behavior, depriving people of enjoyable intimacy and physiological needs.[29]

Ultimately, food and sex are each effective—if potentially problematic—means of distraction or avoidance. The negative impact of using them to soothe pain can infuriate your managerial protectors. Remember, your managers want to maintain an image that controls others' perceptions. If your behavior with food and sex violates family, cultural, or religious rules, you are vulnerable to criticism

---

28. https://www.healthline.com/health/happy-hormone#affection Retrieved on 4/18/23

29. If you were raised in a community that endorsed purity culture, *The Great Sex Rescue: The Lies You've Been Taught and How to Recover What God Intended* by Sheila Gregoire is an invaluable resource.

or ostracism. Your inner critic will likely escalate attacks on your firefighters to shame them into submission.

This internal battle—called a polarity—is a common dynamic in our inner system. Think of it as a tug-of-war between inner family members. Firefighters do what they feel is necessary to squelch a risk, and managers react to the resulting destruction. Managers will berate you about the health effects of overeating, the dangers of sex with strangers, or any other potential threat from a firefighter's strategy. As always, they mean well, and they aren't necessarily wrong. However, shaming the firefighters does not convince them to stop—it may even cause them to escalate their actions. Firefighters will only stop doing what they do when the underlying wound is healed. As the leader of the internal family, you can let both of them know you hear their concerns. Interacting with each of them, one at a time, builds trust in the resources—such as confidence and compassion—your Self offers.

Rage

Anger is one of the primary affective circuits identified by neuroscience.[30] In other words, we are hard-wired to feel anger along with other core emotions such as joy and fear. Anger is an important emotion; it is vital for survival because anger energizes us to confront a threat.

At low levels, we describe anger as irritation or frustration. The rippling in our body alerts us, telling us something is wrong. Maybe there's an imbalance in a relationship; we are doing something someone can and should do for themselves.

If the initial threat isn't resolved, or there's a more significant threat, such as a boundary violation or even unrelenting demands on our time, we will feel angry. Anger tells us to pay attention and take action. Injustice such as racism, misogyny, or the effects of poverty can—and should—make us angry, so we are motivated to do our part to resolve it.

Rage exists at the far end of the spectrum from irritation. It is consuming, white-hot, whole-body energy. When trauma involves a boundary violation such as sexual assault, physical abuse, or even verbal abuse such as bullying, shaming, or demeaning, anger gives us the energy to assert ourselves. If—as is often the

---

30. Jak Panksepp, *Consciousness and Cognition*, Volume 14, Issue 1, March 2005, pg. 30

case—the perpetrator is more powerful than we are, then we cannot use our anger effectively or safely. It stays stuck in our bodies. One horrific episode, or repeated experiences of powerlessness, can deposit a vast reservoir of rage within us. Then, when something activates us, and the exile holding the experience floods the system, a firefighter can use that deposited rage to regain power over the intolerable vulnerability of powerlessness.

As with any of our firefighter strategies, rage erupts with little warning. Your protector is responding to something you might not be consciously aware of. Their response is rapid and intense. Despite their good intentions, acting out of rage leads to physical and emotional harm. Relationships crumble, and sometimes, there can even be criminal ramifications.

It can be challenging to maintain the perspective that part of you believes it has no choice other than rage. It is focused on the threat—such as unbearable powerlessness or weakness—not on the consequences of acting out of rage. But, no matter the impact of their efforts to protect you, they do mean well.

Like other firefighter actions, rage will elicit criticism from your risk managers. They know the pitfalls of allowing rage to lead and will be brutal in chastising you for being out of control. The more extreme the firefighter activity, the more powerful the backlash. This kind of polarity will feel like a fierce, internal battle between bitter enemies. But it is still possible to connect with them, one at a time, to patiently and persistently build trust in the resources Self brings to the system.

Dissociation

Dissociation—disconnecting from both internal and external awareness—is your body's response to overwhelming stress. Have you ever experienced or heard the story of an accident where the person felt disconnected and floating above it, watching it as though it was happening to someone else? When we experience trauma—something "unbearable and intolerable"[31] —the dorsal vagal branch of

---

31. *The Body Keeps the Score: Brain, Mind, and Body in the Healing of Trauma,* Bessel van der Kolk, pg. 1

our autonomic nervous system kicks in. Our system shuts down, and we have "little or no access to thoughts, feelings, or physical sensations."[32]

Can you appreciate how helpful this is? Something our system perceives as life-threatening is happening, and we have the capacity—through dissociation—to completely disconnect from it. It is a grace from God that our bodies can disconnect from warfare, sexual assault and any number of other extreme events, and not be forced to experience the full horror of them.

The challenge arises when part of us uses this strategy frequently because it works so well. Like a complex machine with multiple systems that power down, bringing our systems back online to recover from this utterly detached state takes time. Meanwhile, we miss essential tasks, conversations, and experiences while our faculties are not fully engaged.

If you have a protector who uses dissociation, you could feel their presence as heaviness in your body or a dark cloud that encompasses your inner world. Other parts of you might dislike or fear it because it's powerful. Yet, as with any of our protectors, open-hearted time and attention build a relationship so you can learn what it fears will happen if it doesn't take you out.

Substances and Compulsive Behaviors

Some of the most common tools in your firefighter team's toolbelt are substances and compulsive behaviors that numb pain. When used to excess, things like alcohol, drugs, gambling, and pornography become a means of dealing with overwhelming feelings. Spiritual practices can also be used compulsively to bypass distress.

Because of the physiological impact of substances, they are particularly effective in cutting us off from the tsunami of painful emotions wreaking havoc in our inner system. As is typically the case with firefighters, they act so quickly that we don't realize we've had too much to drink, or used too much of something like cannabis, until we wake up with a pounding head or emerge from a drug-induced fog. The effectiveness of this strategy outweighs the negative consequences; the firefighter using substances is only focused on the threat, not the damage they cause.

---

32. *Transcending Trauma: Healing Complex PTSD with Internal Family Systems Therapy*, Frank G. Anderson, pg. 73

Often, compulsive behaviors provide a positive "hit" that offsets the feelings of despair, hopelessness, and powerlessness carried by our exiles. The reward of winning when gambling or pleasurable sexual sensations are potent, real feelings that relieve distress.

Sadly, temporary relief from painful emotions is often followed by remorse from the impact of the activities. Driving under the influence, incurring debt from gambling, and the health effects of risky sexual behavior are examples of the cost of firefighter activity. Parts of you will be dismayed and critical. Your spouse may not appreciate or care that your pornography use is driven by subconscious firefighters trying to handle the intense pain from your internal wounds. Friends and colleagues who are ignorant of the underlying wounds may also judge destructive behavior. The storm of internal and external criticism can be intense.

When destruction wrought by firefighters incites shame—internally and externally—firefighters will *escalate* their efforts. Shame does nothing to heal underlying wounds; it pours fuel on the fire. Often tragically, firefighters feel they have no choice but to drink *more* or take *more potent* drugs—to do more of what they do because they are desperate for relief.

We saw this dynamic with the Pharisees, who, because of their cultural context, experienced Jesus' ministry as a source of shame; they perceived each radical reinterpretation of what it means to be loving as shameful. What began as confusion escalated to a plot to kill him—to extinguish the source of their pain.

How can you interrupt this desperate and devastating cycle? By turning toward your heroic—yes, *heroic*—firefighters with something they might never have encountered: curiosity. They expect shame and condemnation, and when you meet them with curiosity—asking them to tell you more about how they are trying to help you—they will pause. With sufficient connection, you can offer them what they need most: hope. They need to know there is hope for healing wounds—for freeing your exiles.

Self-Harm, Suicidal Ideation, and Suicide

Self-harm, suicidal ideation, and dying by suicide are three extreme approaches firefighters use when other strategies fail to contain the pain. Self-harm is not the same as a suicide attempt; one does not necessarily lead to the other. I group them because they are not typically the first or second strategy firefighters use. They are like the crew that arrives from a neighboring city during a seven-alarm fire.

In a poignant and beautifully written memoir, Sarah Robinson describes her experience with self-harm. "I despised myself for it, but it was the only way I could let off some of the pressure. The burning sense of badness built up in my chest, and I had to release it somehow. It doesn't make sense if you haven't been there, but the sight of the blood felt like purging some of that pain."[33] Self-harm, whether through cutting, scratching, burning, or other means, releases the pressure of overwhelming pain.

Suicidal ideation—thinking of dying and planning ways to accomplish it—is also a way to relieve the pressure of unbearable suffering. Passive suicidal ideation is common; random thoughts about how much easier it would be to be gone are the first indication that a part of the system is using this means of overcoming distress. Searching the internet for ideas about ways to end your life and fantasizing about carrying out plans is a more active kind of suicidal ideation, reflecting your firefighter's growing concern about the amount of pain in your system. Firefighters who use this means of dousing flames will tell us that they do not want to have to carry out their plans—but if the pain is too great, they will act. When a client has this kind of firefighter, we prioritize building a relationship with them. It is vital to engage with them to offer hope for healing.

Tragically, excruciating suffering can lead to death by suicide. The torment of misery eclipses the hope that things can change. Beliefs that you are too much for the people you love, that they will be better off without you, that you are broken and forsaken, feel true. And part of you knows how to end your anguish. So it takes action.

If one of your loved ones has died by suicide, I am so sorry. This is a complex loss, and trying to understand it—let alone grieving it—can challenge your internal system and activate your own protectors. Unanswerable questions and unbearable what-ifs deserve your attention and compassion. I hope understanding and connecting with your inner family members supports your grief process.

---

33. *I Love Jesus But I Want to Die: Finding Hope in the Darkness of Depression,* Sarah J. Robinson, pg. 27

Are Protective Strategies Sinful?

We have a God-given ability to adapt to survive and continue to develop despite experiencing distressing and terrible things. It is crucial for your healing journey to understand that symptoms and behaviors you might feel shame about or are desperate to resolve began as an adaptive response to overwhelming events. This perspective opens space for compassion and curiosity—vital resources parts need to feel if they are going to trust the Self as a companion for healing.

Curiosity allows us to turn toward protectors with a sincere desire to hear their stories. They are motivated by fear—primarily that we will be overwhelmed with emotional pain if they don't control, numb, or distract us. Their focus is on our exiles, and their jobs are a valiant effort to contain or mitigate pain. When we separate motivation from effect, space opens for connection. Understanding the positive intentions driving protectors can even inspire gratitude.

However, the protective strategies we examined are frequently shamed and judged by other parts—or other people—as sinful. The difficulty is not with the label "sin;" the difficulty is the intention behind the label. Are we naming something sin to inspire curiosity about why a behavior persists or to face a challenge courageously? Or, are we calling something sin out of a desire to distance ourselves from someone's pain—to feel powerful rather than powerless? Our protectors shy away from vulnerability and will use judgment and shame to control parts of us and others.

What if the religious leaders had chosen to approach Jesus with curiosity, as Nicodemus did?[34] Nicodemus was a Pharisee who would have shared some of our fictional Eli's concerns. But instead of keeping his distance and allowing fear to drive his actions, he approached Jesus with curiosity, which enabled him to draw closer to Jesus and begin understanding who he was. He encouraged other Pharisees to interact with Jesus rather than condemning him based on their judgment about what he was doing.

This is how we must interact with our protectors; shame and judgment block healing and break relationships—internally and externally. Remembering that the behaviors, thoughts, emotions, and impulses we call "sin" are adaptive responses

34. John 3:1-21, John 7:50-51.

to suffering is vital. We "sin" in response to adversity because protectors act independently of our sources of wisdom—Self and Spirit. This perspective builds a bridge to a part of us who needs loving attention.

Doug Frank writes, "The freedom to be a mess—to be accepting of and present to every part of us, no matter how 'shabby,' 'disreputable,' or 'troublesome'—is the heart of the Christian understanding of wholeness."[35] We cannot be whole if we reject parts of ourselves. Healing is a process of restoring harmony in our internal system—freeing each member to contribute the qualities they were created to contribute.

Does that mean we ignore the impact of protective strategies? Not at all. Their impact is an alarm bell alerting us to wounds requiring healing. But it is crucial to separate protectors' actions from their essence. If we look beyond behavior—and the ramifications of it—we can approach protectors with understanding. We will learn they are burdened by the job they feel they have no choice but to perform on behalf of our internal family. We can join them in grieving the impact of their efforts to protect us and reassure them that healing is possible.

Befriending protectors instills hope, and hope is a soothing elixir. Validating their efforts, appreciating their intentions, and helping them see that they do not have to be bound by roles they adopted out of necessity—not choice—enables them to relax. Protectors begin to trust the Self because they experience the impact of the resources the Self brings to the system. And as capacity for Self-leadership grows, Self can give us the courage we need to face the external consequences of our actions, and the creativity and connection needed to begin cleaning up any messes we have made in our families and friendships.

Ultimately, with sufficient trust in Self-leadership, our protectors will grant access to the most vulnerable members of your internal family—the ones holding pain. Safely entering stories riddled with pain is the next phase of our journey to *shalom*.

---

35. *A Gentler God: Breaking Free of the Almighty in the Presence of the Human Jesus*, Doug Frank, pg. 376

Spiritual Practice: Identifying and Befriending Firefighters

We use a similar approach to connecting with firefighters as with other protectors. You don't have to distinguish between proactive managers and reactive firefighters, so please don't worry about "getting it right." As you develop relationships with members of your inner family, their roles and relationships will become clearer.

Did the descriptions of typical firefighters alert you to a reactive protector in your internal family? If not, recall an incident where you said or did something you later regretted. Maybe you were mystified by how quickly you reacted. Bringing that incident to mind can help you identify a firefighter in your system. Then you can use the same steps you learned in chapter six to connect with them. I repeat those steps below for convenience.

Awareness of a Reactive Protector—A Firefighter

- Notice your inner experience, including sensations, thoughts, emotions, and images.
- If you feel overwhelmed, breathe deeply, and exhale slowly. Imagine your breath creating a healing space for connection.
- What feels most intense? Bring your attention to it.
- You've just identified a member of your internal family!
    - Where are they located in your body?
    - What emotions do they hold?
    - Do you see them?
- You can pause here and make a note in your journal about this valuable member of your internal family.

Unblending—Differentiating Between the Self and the Protector

- Return to the protector you identified. You are ready to continue connecting with them when you sense their presence (through their emotions, thoughts, or sensations).

- Ask yourself, "***How am I feeling toward this part of me?***"

    - We ask this because there are many members of your internal family, but you can only connect with one at a time. Remember the metaphor of a director working with actors on a stage. You want to shine the spotlight on one member of the cast of characters while others wait in the wings for their turn.

    - In response to the question, "How am I feeling toward it?" you might hear, "I'm afraid of it," "I don't like it," or "I'm annoyed by it." Or, your heart is racing, your breath is shallow, or there's an impulse to run.

    - Anything *other than* one of the 8 Cs (or some other manifestation of love) means that other parts are present. Remind them that you value their input, but can only connect with one part at a time. Ask them to give you space, and let them know you will connect with them when it's their turn.

    - Because firefighters will do whatever it takes to extinguish the flame of pain, their activity often provokes criticism from other members of the internal family. You might need to get to know a critical part—and validate its concerns—before you can connect or move further with the firefighter.

- Now, notice how you are feeling toward the original firefighting part. Are you at least somewhat curious and open to connecting? You do not have to be 100% Self-led; we just need sufficient Self-energy to create a safe and trusting bond.

- Note your response to this firefighting part of you in your journal. Which

"C" quality does it inspire? How does it feel to realize their activity is not your whole identity? What happens in your inner system as you imagine befriending them and working together, rather than them toiling alone or being criticized by other parts of you?

Befriending The Firefighter

- The next step is ***befriending*** (the heart of this practice).
- Some helpful questions to get you started:
    - How are you trying to help me?
    - Do you like your job?
    - How long have you been doing it?
    - What do you need from me?
- Remember that this is a relationship, not an interrogation, so notice the response to your questions. Some parts aren't very verbal. Their response could be a shift in sensations or emotions. You will be able to tell whether they are open to connecting with you or whether they are reluctant.
- If the part of you is not responsive, or is snarky, remember they might have been toiling on behalf of the inner system for years without any recognition or assistance—or despite others criticizing them for what they do. Let them know you appreciate their efforts!
- You can also ask questions to assess how they view you:
    - Do you trust I am here to help you?
    - What would help you trust me more?
- Whenever the current conversation is complete, thank them for being willing to connect. Let them know you would like to continue the conversation.

- Jot some notes in your journal about how it felt to get to know this prominent member of your inner family. How did they initially respond? What happened as you remained connected and curious? How do you feel about committing to an ongoing relationship? What emotions arise as you think of this new acquaintance?

Deepening the Relationship

Befriending parts of you takes time and intention. When you think of this process as developing a relationship with a part of you who works diligently to protect you, it will feel like an opportunity rather than a task.

- When you return to the firefighter, ask again, "How am I feeling toward them?"
    - It is helpful to note other parts who are present. Often, the same ones will show up. For example, if you meet with a firefighter who uses food or substances to soothe pain, you might also notice a part criticizing them for "being out of control."
    - Ask the critical part to give you space, but let them know you'd also like to meet with them. Because firefighters provoke criticism, fear, and shaming, balancing connecting with a firefighter and their opponent is essential.
- As you meet with each protector, notice their response. Do you feel you've made a new friend? Do they trust that you have something valuable to offer?
- Spend time getting to know their job, how they feel about it, and extending appreciation for their role.
- Jot notes in your journal about your interactions with each member of your inner family.

Building Awareness of "Polarities"

As we discussed, a "polarity" in your inner system is a tug-of-war between two parts of you. Protectors can be polarized; they have different ideas about how to help you avoid an exile's pain.

- As you reflect on your internal family system, are you aware of a polarity—a tug-of-war—between a part whose activity is impulsive (a firefighter) and another who blames and criticizes you for it (a manager)? Both of them fear you'll be overwhelmed by shame if they fail to control or numb pain.
    - For example, if you drink or eat more than you intended, or spend hours watching shows, do you notice a part of you who criticizes you afterwards? The one who over-indulges is trying to numb pain, and the critical part wants to control the firefighter.
- Protectors have jobs—whether impulsive or controlling—because they are trying to numb or avoid pain held by an exile. The exile holds shame from experiences that left them feeling defective.
- Draw a triangle with your manager, firefighter and exile. It is an upside-down triangle, with opposing protectors at the top and an exile at the point on the bottom.
- What do you notice as you consider the relationship between these inner family members? Do you feel Self-energy—one of the 8 Cs, the "P" of perspective—or the loving energy of the Spirit as you consider how much pain your exile might be holding, and how diligently your protectors work to help you get through life despite it?
- If helpful for deepening your connection, depict each part with an object, a photo, or a drawing.
- Consider how God is present with each participant in this triangle.
    - How would God love the part who blames the firefighter for

wreaking havoc?

  - What would God say to the firefighter who will do whatever it takes to numb the terrible pain?

  - Imagine the Presence of Love holding your vulnerable exile.

- If you discover new members of your inner family, make a note in your journal so you can return to them and deepen the relationship.

Connecting with Your Inner Pharisee

Judgment is one of the strategies protectors use to distance us from pain—our own or others'. It's uncomfortable to admit how often these protectors constrain Self-energy and how often we lead with judgment rather than love. Befriending your judgmental protector is an impactful step in healing. I encourage you to use the process above to connect with the part(s) of you who judge others. You might notice another part of you who feels guilt or shame about how often the judgmental part of you surfaces. Reassure them that your inner "Pharisee" means well and that building a relationship with them will help them trust your ability to handle distress.

Chapter Eight

The Stories We Hide

2 Samuel 13:1-22

The following story is about the rape of Tamar by her half-brother, Amnon. Please be mindful of whether this is a good time to read something that could be activating. Take a moment and shift your attention inside. What do you feel in your body as you anticipate reading about incest and sexual assault? If any part of you is distressed, extend loving-kindness and ask what they need. Honor their wishes.

Amnon thought of nothing else. Tamar's beauty captivated him, and his desire for her tormented him. His heart raced, and his body burned when he imagined lying with her. Agitated, he paced like a caged lion. Amnon felt sick with longing and was obsessed with trying to figure out how to have her.[1]

But Tamar, his half-sister, was a virgin, and it seemed impossible to get her alone.[2] She was always with the other daughters of the king, carefully shielded from men—even relatives.

After tossing and turning through another long, sleepless night, Amnon's friend Jonadab asked him why he looked so haggard. Amnon confessed, "I'm in love with Tamar, my brother Absalom's sister."[3] A shrewd man, Jonadab quickly devised a plan to help his friend get what he wanted. He said, "Go to bed and pretend to be ill. When your father comes to see you, say to him, 'I would like my sister Tamar to come and give me something to eat. Let her prepare the food in my sight so I may watch her and then eat it from her hand.'"[4]

---

1. 2 Samuel 13:2, NIV

2. 2 Samuel 13:2, NIV

3. 2 Samuel 13:4, NIV

4. 2 Samuel 13:5, NIV

Amnon was elated! What a brilliant plan. As King David's firstborn son, Amnon always got whatever he wanted. Finally, he would also have Tamar.

Tamar was concerned when her father, King David, asked her to care for Amnon. Surely he must be very ill if the king wanted his sister—rather than his servants—to feed him. She hurried to his house and prepared bread for him. But when it was ready, Amnon refused to get out of bed to eat. He ordered the servants to leave and commanded Tamar to come into his bedroom to feed him herself.[5] Tamar was puzzled, wondering if he was too ill to leave his bed, so she did as he told her.

When Amnon grabbed her and said, "Come to bed with me, my sister," Tamar felt bile rise in her throat. His intense gaze made her skin crawl. Muscles rigid with fear, Tamar begged Amnon to come to his senses. "Don't force me! Such a thing should not be done in Israel! Don't do this wicked thing!"[6]

Tamar saw the lust in his eyes and knew he did not care about violating their moral code. So she begged her brother to see her as a person—to see her as his sister, not an object for his pleasure. "What about me? Where could I get rid of my shame?"[7]

Amnon turned away—unwilling to look at her as she desperately grasped for something to stop him. Clearly, he cared nothing about how this would affect her, so Tamar pivoted. "What about you? You would be like one of the wicked fools in Israel."[8]

Amnon's silence was terrifying. Tamar felt a cold sweat break out, and panic made it hard to breathe. Desperate to avoid something she could barely tolerate imagining, she pleaded with Amnon to ask the king to allow them to be married.[9] She loathed the idea of being this brute's wife, but at least she would have the dignity of marriage.

---

5. 2 Samuel 13:9-10, NIV

6. 2 Samuel 13:11-12, NIV

7. 2 Samuel 13:13, NRSV

8. 2 Samuel 13:13, NIV

9. 2 Samuel 13:13, NIV

Her words were like throwing pebbles at a raging bear. When Amnon grabbed her and threw her on the bed, Tamar squeezed her eyes shut. His strength thwarted every attempt she made to fight back. He took what he wanted; he raped her.[10]

Tamar felt like it was happening to someone else, as though a cold fog separated her from herself. Part of her hoped to stay in the fog, floating and disconnected from reality. But awareness crept in, and hot shame dispelled the fog. Her limbs were leaden; she wanted to curl up and weep.

Another part of her was desperate to get away from him. Dizzy from the pain wracking her body, she began to straighten her clothing. And then, when she thought she had suffered the worst thing imaginable, Amnon inflicted more pain. His face contorted by hatred and disgust, he said, "Get up and get out!"[11]

Finding strength she didn't know she had, Tamar said, "No! Sending me away would be a greater wrong than what you have already done to me!"[12] Banishing her would be the final proof that she was just an object of lust, not a person for whom Amnon felt any affection.

But the heat of his pursuit had given way to ice-cold hostility. Amnon called his servant and said, "Get this woman out of my sight and bolt the door after her."[13]

Shame flooded Tamar's body, and her legs buckled. The servant reached out to keep her from falling, and she was mortified that he witnessed her degradation.

Head down, she stumbled through the kitchen. Tamar tore her robe and put ashes from the fire on her head, announcing her loss. Consumed by injustice and grief, Tamar wailed as she trudged to her brother Absalom's house.[14]

Tamar dared to hope Absalom would acknowledge the wrong done to her when Absalom asked, "Has that Amnon, your brother, been with you?" Tamar began to share her story, but before she could string coherent words together, Absalom

---

10. 2 Samuel 13:14, NIV

11. 2 Samuel 13:15, NIV

12. 2 Samuel 13:16, NIV

13. 2 Samuel 13:17, NIV

14. 2 Samuel 13:19, NIV

silenced her. "Be quiet for now, my sister; he is your brother. Don't take this thing to heart."[15]

Be quiet? Don't take it to heart? Don't protest being violated and stripped of my future?! Her brother's complicity in a code of silence magnified her half-brother's betrayal.

While Absalom would eventually exact revenge, Amnon obliterated Tamar's future. From then on, she "lived in her brother Absalom's house, a desolate woman."[16]

An Exile is Born

Tamar's story takes us into the most vulnerable territory of our inner terrain—where exiles live.

A father she trusted sent her to a half-brother she trusted, and when he raped her, she went to another trusted brother for refuge. Every one of them failed her. A young virgin, she would have expected life to include marriage and a family. Instead, she was brutalized and thrown out like rotten garbage. Dreams shattered, family bonds severed, and trust in herself and others lost, Tamar represents the wounded, burdened members of the inner family cut off from love and security.

Tamar's desperate—yet creative and courageous—attempts to fight for herself reveal the person shattered by the impact of trauma. In her valiant struggle, she draws on God-given resources to stave off disaster. She invoked morality and culture; "Such a thing should not be done in Israel!" When that failed, her plea was for compassion. "Where could I get rid of my shame?" She knew the future that awaited her if Amnon succeeded. I imagine she sensed the futility of relying on his compassion as she quickly pivoted to his ego. "You would be like one of the wicked fools in Israel." Surely that would get his attention! But the privileged life of the king's first-born son insulated him from believing there would be consequences for his behavior; after all, his father took what he wanted with impunity. Tamar acquiesced to reality, saying, "Please speak to the king; he will not keep me from being married to you." Tragically, despite her efforts, she was not able to sway Amnon. Powerlessness, shame, and grief replaced courage and confidence.

---

15. 2 Samuel 13:20, NIV

16. 2 Samuel 13:20, NIV

As is often the case, secondary trauma—being banished by Amnon and having her experience invalidated by Absalom—compounded the impact of the traumatic event. While the text says King David was "furious," and Absalom ultimately had Amnon killed, there was no justice for Tamar.[17] Tamar lived out her life in exile, a desolate woman—barren, wretched, abandoned, forlorn.

Trauma and Adversity Create Exiles

Tamar's story reveals the complex interplay of events and wounds characteristic of adverse or traumatic experiences. Her story begins with a betrayal of trust, as is true of any interpersonal violation—from misattuned caregivers across the spectrum to violent perpetrators. Trust is the air relationships breathe; when violated, the impact feels like suffocation. Because relationships—from casual to intimate—rely on trust, if betrayal shatters trust, the part of us who experiences betrayal is untethered. The tie that binds us to other humans is broken for that member of our internal family.

Cast adrift from the safety of connection, they feel the panic of abandonment and the shame of rejection. Powerlessness and despair replace their sense of self-efficacy. Distorted beliefs of their defectiveness and worthlessness erase confidence in their value. Hopelessness prevails, and grief over incalculable loss consumes.

Is it any wonder betrayal provokes an array of protective strategies among inner family members? They must exile the part of you carrying the devastating impact of betrayal because their pain presents too great a risk to the system.

All of us have exiles in our inner family. The pain they carry depends on the meaning we made of the events they endured. It is impossible to apply an "objective" evaluation to determine what we "should" feel as a result of adversity. Temperament, context, the quality of our relationships, prior experiences, and many other variables affect the meaning we make of events. Our practice is to connect with exiles to learn *from them* about their burdens.

Building awareness of our exiles is a crucial step in our healing process. Orienting ourselves to different types of adverse events and the emotions and beliefs they prompt helps us attune to their presence in our internal system.

---

17. 2 Samuel 13:21, 32, NIV

Events that Create Exiles

Across our lifespan, we are vulnerable to experiencing betrayal and rejection—from early experiences with caregivers, to shifting alliances in middle school friend groups, to infidelity, abuse or assault. Betrayal affects our ability to trust others and ourselves. We wonder how we can trust someone after betrayal and how we can trust ourselves—because we "should" have known they weren't trustworthy. We are vulnerable to distorted beliefs such as, "I'm unlovable," "I'm worthless," or "It's my fault." Our expectations of safety, loving-kindness, or respect are dashed. Our view of the world and our place in it shifts, sometimes radically, which is disorienting and confusing. Significant relationships are ruptured, prompting anxiety, loneliness, and even panic. Rejection by a peer group or important person is threatening because it disrupts the emotional safety of loving connection. Anticipating support and being met with invalidating or minimizing reactions further undermines security. Much is lost as a result of betrayal and rejection.

In addition to betrayal, other losses are inevitable. Loved ones die, marriages end, physical and mental illness strike, careers shift, and financial security sometimes ebbs. While loss can provoke an array of emotions, including anxiety, loneliness, anger, hopelessness, and despair, it inevitably leads to grief. Unresolved losses and repressed grief do not dissipate with time. If cultural rules or circumstances conspire to constrain the grief process, the weight of sadness burdens exiles.

Traumatic events such as sexual assault, abuse, and myriad forms of violence engender powerlessness and helplessness. Advocating for needs and exercising choice are fundamental human rights that trauma erases. A perpetrator with personal and systemic power violates an individual's agency and integrity. A man who rapes reflects the ultimate cost of patriarchy—the view of women as objects to be used by men. Political systems give rise to tyrants and dictators whose quest for power rationalizes war. Sexual abuse by clergy occurs in systems prioritizing charismatic leaders and growth over transparency and accountability. A twisted, fear-driven pursuit of power and security condones violence against marginalized people.

Judith Herman, a renowned trauma expert, highlights how systemic and cultural norms compound adversity's effects. For example, one sexual assault survivor she interviewed shared how "everyday sexism," such as hearing men talk about going to strip clubs and viewing pornography, became "intolerable" after she experienced sexual violence.[18] Consider how "everyday" racism, homo- and transphobia, and dehumanization of ethnic minorities impact individuals; systemic messages that reinforce feelings of worthlessness compound interpersonal wounds. Passivity regarding an epidemic of gun violence must mystify and enrage people whose family members died in shootings.

A related phenomenon, the role of bystanders, is another example of the layered experience of adversity. Bystanders can be actively or passively complicit.[19] People at a party who do nothing to protect an inebriated woman's safety or pedestrians who turn away as a person experiencing homelessness is assaulted lend credence to a person's belief that they are defective. And it adds fuel to the fire when a victim turns to someone for support and their concerns are invalidated, or an abuser's actions are minimized or tacitly condoned.

Are you wondering whether your distressing experiences were "bad enough" to cause protectors to exile parts of you? After all, maybe you had "good enough" parents who provided shelter, food, and a reasonably consistent amount of attention and support. You didn't suffer abuse as a child, and you haven't experienced a traumatic event. If that's the case, I'm glad!

And yet. Ask yourself whether you have any protective strategies—minimizing your own or others' pain, avoiding emotional vulnerability, and criticizing yourself and others, to name a few of the most common ones. Did you resonate with any protective strategies I covered in chapters six and seven? Parts of us adopt protective roles to avoid or numb pain. No matter how much good we experience, I think it's impossible to live on this planet and be impervious to pain. Even "routine" events—such as being picked last for a team, feeling like an outsider, having your heart broken, and losing the comparison game—can burden parts of you with pain. Pain threatens your well-being, so protectors will have jobs to deal with it. Remember, the meaning we make of our experiences is highly subjective and is informed by *implicit* memories held in our subconscious.

---

18. *Truth and Repair: How Trauma Survivors Envision Justice,* Judith Herman, pg. 11

19. Ibid, pg. 79

Experiences that challenge our identity as Beloved vary in intensity and effect, yet, they have one thing in common: they induce shame.

Shame

Tamar's only personal reference to the impact of rape was to ask, "As for me, where could I carry my shame?"[20] She knew Amnon's betrayal would render her an outcast, left alone to carry the burden of brokenness.

Shame is isolating because it follows a rupture of a trusted relationship. Psychiatrist and trauma expert Dr. Frank Anderson says, "Shame develops when vulnerability is relationally violated."[21] Humans are inherently vulnerable; we depend on loving connections for healthy functioning. Acts that disregard, disrupt, or disrespect our humanity inflict a profound wound. Shame is the emotional response to rejection, ridicule, or ostracism.[22]

Relational rupture—whether through a pattern with caregivers of misattunement, neglect, or criticism, experiences of being an outsider, or the violation of personal integrity inherent in racism, bullying, domestic violence, abuse, and assault—is interpreted as defectiveness. The meaning made of experiences provoking shame is that they happened *because* we are worthless, stupid, or unlovable. If I mattered and had value, those things would not have happened to me. The story a part of us holds is that we are "deserted, forgotten, dismissed, scorned, pushed out, abandoned."[23] When we believe rejection is a reflection of our worth, we will feel the intensely painful emotion of shame.

Shame appears to be uniquely human. It is not one of the seven primary emotional circuits we have in common with other mammals, as identified by neuroscientist Jaak Panksepp. Curt Thompson, in his excellent exploration of shame, provides an explanation, "No one ever feels the sharp sting of shame apart

---

20. 2 Samuel 13:13, NRSV

21. *Transcending Trauma: Healing Complex PTSD with Internal Family Systems Therapy*, Frank G. Anderson, pg. 109

22. *Truth and Repair: How Trauma Survivors Envision Justice*, Judith Herman, pg. 32

23. *The Soul of Shame: Retelling the Stories We Believe About Ourselves*, Curt Thompson, pg 54

from an initial encounter with someone else that...activates the shame response."[24] Shame is interpersonal.

For a young child, disapproval or criticism can foster shame.[25] If disapproval were to rise to the level of abandonment, we could actually die. Thus, disapproval is risky for our survival, and our nervous system is vigilant about such risks. It makes sense that our emotional system registers disapproval so strongly when we are young. We doubt our worth when there is a pattern of condescension, sarcasm, teasing, or irritation in significant relationships.

The absence of attention characteristic of neglect also fuels shame. When an important person is unavailable, preoccupied, or emotionally detached, that, too, is experienced as abandonment. It is easy to see how a child who persistently lacks connection would decide, "I'm unlovable" or "I'm unworthy."

We feel relational ruptures leading to shame in our bodies. There is a sense of collapse, of turning in on ourselves; we avoid eye contact, our face is flushed, and we notice an impulse to hide. Our stomach aches, our chest is heavy, and we feel deflated.[26] Louis Cozolino, a psychotherapist who has authored many books about interpersonal neurobiology, notes that when we are shamed, we shift from "curiosity, exploration, and excitement...to shutdown and withdrawal." He calls these shifts "mini-traumas" because they "stimulate the same regions of the brain that are activated during pain."[27] Shame registers as physical pain.

Painful shame blocks innate confidence in our worth; it silences our voice. At a time when we most need loving connection, shame keeps us from reaching for it. It is a barrier—a bunker in which a part of us hides from what now feels like a hostile world. I think of Tamar, hidden away from the world, cut off from her hopes and dreams, living with the shame no one helped her heal.

If shame is such a debilitating emotion, why do we have it? What purpose does it serve—other than to cause misery? Allan Schore, one of the eminent

---

24. Ibid, pg. 69

25. Ibid, pg. 62 (quoting Michael Lewis, *Shame: The Exposed Self*, pg 91-94)

26. *Parenting from the Inside Out: How a Deeper Self-Understanding Can Help You Raise Children Who Thrive,* Daniel J. Siegel and Mary Hartzell, pg. 222

27. Louis Cozolino, *The Neuroscience of Human Relationships: Attachment and the Developing Social Brain*, in *Transcending Trauma*, Frank G. Anderson, pg. 114

neuroscientists of our time, says shame "perhaps more than any other emotion is intimately tied to the physiological expression of the stress response...This underscores...the function of shame as an arousal blocker. Shame reduces self-exposure or self-exploration."[28] Shame serves a *protective* function. If our environment is unsafe, shame quiets us, inhibiting spontaneity, playfulness, exuberance, and assertiveness. Shame inspires submission in contexts where confidence elicits punishment—thwarting behavior that generates angry or abusive reactions by caregivers or other authority figures.

Broken relationships deposit a reservoir of shame in our internal system, and parts of us use shame to avoid risking further pain. The load of shame you carry can feel like muck in a swamp that sucks you in as you desperately try to escape it. Thankfully, there is hope; there is a path out of the swamp.

Relationships Wound and Relationships Heal

Imagine exiles cut off from nurturing care for what is often many, many years. They have felt the influence of protectors who dislike or fear them and perhaps the occasional frisson of affection from a protector who is a caregiver. But they have not seen loving eyes whose gaze penetrates the gloom with the light of hope. They have not felt the warmth of a gentle, patient presence whose reassurance that they matter contradicts beliefs of worthlessness. Confidence, hope, and courage have not reassured them that their story isn't over.

They have not met *you*.

They have not been held in a sacred space where your Self joins the Spirit in welcoming them just as they are, wounded and weary.

That is the next step on our journey to *shalom*: the initial connection with an exile to let them know Love is present, Love is for them, and Love can support them in releasing their burdens. In the following chapter, we will unpack the complete process of healing, but for now, I encourage you to practice simply cultivating awareness of your inner family's most tender and vulnerable members. You can learn to meet them in the sacred space where Love begins to dissolve barriers to their belovedness.

---

28. *Affect Regulation and the Repair of the Self,* Allan N. Schore, pg. 154

Spiritual Practice: Building Awareness of Your Exiles

Your exiles hold intense emotions such as shame, grief, despair, and terror. Protectors fear you will be overwhelmed by these emotions, but in the presence of Self, exiles do not have to flood you with pain because they trust they have your attention. Therefore, you must be Self-and-Spirit-led when connecting with exiles. That is often not possible on your own. Please respect your protectors and do not try to force an exile into the open! It is almost *always* the case that you will need support from a trained IFS professional in connecting with exiles, as their level of pain is simply too great for our nervous system to let us remain in a ventral vagal state (remaining Self-led) as exiles unburden their shame.[29] The importance of a trained and trusted professional is not simply about technique or knowledge of the process; their presence and attention is a very real resource to your body and inner world.

That being said, I offer the following exercises for several reasons. One is that sometimes exiles unexpectedly surface and flood your system, and I want you to know how to bring Self-energy to the exile to calm your system. Second, some readers will have experience working with IFS professionals and might have developed sufficient trust with protectors to be able to do more work on their own with exiles. If that's you, I want to equip you with a practice you can use. Finally, knowing the approach will provide a vision and practical preparation for a future therapeutic relationship, when it is suitable for you to find a professional.

The following exercise helps build awareness of Self-energy, and can fill your inner system with Self-energy when you feel open to connecting with exiles.[30]

---

29. You can find an IFS therapist in your area through the IFS Institute website: https://ifs-institute.com/practitioners

30. This is a modified version of The Path exercise in *No Bad Parts: Healing Trauma & Restoring Wholeness with The Internal Family Systems Model* by Richard C. Schwartz, PhD, pg. 93

Experiencing the Presence of Self

- Imagine a space holding all the parts you know. It can be a cozy living room with a fire in the fireplace, a library stocked with your favorite books, or a meadow in the sunshine—whatever you imagine would be a welcoming space for your internal family.

- Once they are present, let them know you are going for a walk. Reassure them you won't be gone long and won't forget them; if they get concerned, they can call you back. You will hear them.

- If any part of you is unwilling to allow you to leave, connect with them instead. You can try this exercise another time.

- When all parts are willing, imagine walking in your favorite outdoor area. Are you by a river or the ocean? What's the temperature? Notice the air—moist or dry, fragrant or crisp. What do you hear?

- If your mind is busy with thoughts, there are still some parts with you. Ask them to return to the room, and reassure them you'll return soon.

- Now shift your awareness to your body. Notice the presence of Self: calm, quiet mind, spacious heart, relaxed belly. Do you feel the energy of creativity or courage? Is there freedom to be in the moment?

- How is God present with you—in Creation, as a warm presence, in the wind?

- As you walk, you might notice that some parts have joined you—you're feeling anxious, there's tension in your body, or thoughts have taken a distressing turn. Ask them gently to return to the room.

    - If a part is persistent, ask what they fear will happen if they stay behind and let you take your walk. Reassure them that you are not abandoning them.

- At some point in your walk, pause to notice what it feels like when the

Self is filling your body. It will feel spacious and relaxed inside. A sense of well-being, connection with God, and even vibrating or glowing energy are common evidence of Self. Allow yourself time to revel in the presence of God within you.

- When you're ready, return to the room where you left your parts.

- Ask your parts what it was like for them. Thank them for allowing you to take your walk. If it feels natural, share some qualities you enjoyed—curiosity, calm, patience, or confidence—whatever you experienced. Let them know these God-given resources are available to them, and you will meet with each of them as they need you to help them.

Inviting Exiles into a Sacred Space for Connection

When we turn toward our exiles, we invite the most vulnerable parts of us to be known. They have not felt the warmth of a gentle, patient presence whose assurance that they matter contradicts beliefs of worthlessness. They have not met your Self, and so their prior experience of "who you were" was unsafe. Accordingly, we must approach them with gentleness, at a pace that establishes trust. As always, we respect our protectors by acknowledging them and inviting them to allow the Self to lead. It will be particularly helpful to make notes about the members of your internal family that you encounter as you enter into more vulnerable spaces.

- Shift your attention inside.

- Ask yourself, *"How am I feeling toward the part of me whose presence brings shame, grief, terror, or a sense of my defectiveness into awareness?*

- It is rare that vulnerable members of your inner family surface without provoking some of your protectors. They will constrain loving kindness, so take your time noticing if there's hesitation, fear, irritation, or anything *other than* curiosity, confidence, and compassion.

- Sometimes, a protector is a caregiver who wants to help your exile. You might see this part of you holding your exile. If you can see a part, it is not the Self. (You cannot see Self as you see parts; Self is the one who sees with the eyes of Love. For example, when you hold a child, you cannot see your own face.) Thank them for their concern, and ask them to allow you to lead. They can remain nearby.

- When you feel curious and confident about connecting with a wounded member of your inner family, turn toward them and let them know you care about them.

- At this time, you are just practicing being with them. Notice how they respond to your presence, and accept their response without pressuring them to change.

- Is your heart open to them? Allow loving energy to flow from your heart to theirs.

- Ask if there's anything they need to feel safe. They might want to invite the Spirit, Jesus, or some other trusted person to be with them. Allow them to lead. While the Self holds hope for healing, when the Self leads, there is no pressure or agenda forcing change.

- Let them know you intend to help them unload their burdens. Record this interaction in your journal so you can return to your exile at the appropriate time.

- Protectors can return and block healing energy at any point in this process. You might become distracted, foggy, or sleepy. Perhaps a critical part of you lobs insults at the exile. When you notice a protector's presence, ask them to step back; reassure them you have what the exile needs. If they are persistent, shift your focus to them and use practices in chapters six and seven to connect with them.

Chapter Nine

Tell Me the Whole Story

John 11:1-44

Lazarus sensed the presence of his sisters, and he longed to connect with them. But pain muddled his mind; he couldn't find words to express his longing. As fever ravaged his body and his strength ebbed, he felt cut off from the outside world. The agony of fear and grief encapsulated him.

Mary's heart pounded with alarm; Lazarus was delirious. He mumbled words, but they made no sense. She said, "Martha! He's worse this morning! We need to send for help!"

Martha ran next door and asked a neighbor to take a message to Jesus. "Tell Jesus, the one you love is sick."[1]

Martha returned, finding Mary weeping. She said, "Sister, Jesus can heal our brother. Every time he visits us, there are new examples of his power to heal. Surely, he will come to help his dear friend."[2]

The sisters grew increasingly concerned as the hours ticked by. They tried to cling to the hope that Jesus would arrive in time, but Lazarus was restless, and his skin was grey and clammy. He grew quiet and still. As dawn broke, he took his final breath.

Mary's cry echoed through the quiet village. As she wept over her brother's body, Martha pushed her grief down and began preparing the household for formal mourning.[3]

---

1. John 11:3, NIV

2. A commentator suggests Mary, Martha, and Lazarus may have become an extended family for Jesus. Gary M. Burge, The NIV Application Commentary: John, pg. 312.

3. See Luke 10:38 for a description of the different personalities of the two sisters.

A neighbor came to inquire about Lazarus, and Martha asked him to spread the word. Throughout the day, people arrived from around the area crying and wailing loudly.[4]

Martha and Mary prepared Lazarus for burial, tenderly wrapping his body in strips of cloth filled with burial spices. Saying their final goodbyes, they covered his face with a piece of linen.

Men from the village carried Lazarus' body to the tomb, a cave cut into the hillside, and rolled the stone across the entrance.[5]

The day after the sisters sent him, their friend reached Jesus to share the news about Lazarus. Jesus was concerned—dear friends were suffering—but he reassured everyone that the illness would not end in death.[6]

As Jesus prepared to return to Judea, his disciples expressed apprehension. "But Rabbi, a short while ago, people there tried to stone you, and yet you are going back?"[7] Jesus reassured them that nothing would stop him from being able to help Lazarus; God's love would prevail.

Martha met them on the road as they neared Bethany. Her face told the story of the last few days, and Jesus' heart ached for her. Her faith was touching; Jesus grieved her regret as she said, "Lord, if you had been here, my brother would not have died. But I know that even now God will give you whatever you ask."[8] He comforted her and asked her to bring Mary to him.

The crowd of mourners followed Mary. When she reached Jesus, she fell at his feet weeping and said, "Lord, if you had been here, my brother would not have died."[9] Jesus felt Mary's pain as it rippled through the group grieving for Lazarus. His gut clenched, and anger rose. He was outraged at the bitter cost of

---

4. See Mark 5:38 and Matthew 9:23. Mourning was a communal event. Gary M. Burge, The NIV Application Commentary: John, pg. 315

5. For a description of a typical Judean tomb, see Gary M. Burge, The NIV Application Commentary: John, pg. 315

6. John 11:4, NIV

7. John 11:8, paraphrase.

8. John 11:21-22, NIV

9. John 11:32, NIV

death.[10] It was time to show these dear people that love triumphs over the ultimate injustice: death. Jesus, choking back tears of frustration,[11] said, "Where have you laid him?"[12]

Seeing the stone covering the tomb, Jesus felt a renewed upwelling of indignation.[13] He allowed himself to feel the devastating impact of loss—the terrible toll of the ultimate exile from all of the goodness God intends for his beloved children. Enough of this suffering! Jesus said, "Take away the stone."[14]

Martha was stunned; didn't Jesus realize how long the body had been in the tomb? Gathering the courage to challenge Jesus, she said, "But Lord, by this time, there is a bad odor, for he has been there four days."[15]

Jesus looked lovingly at Martha, his friend who was always taking care of others. He took her hands in his and reminded her of what he told her earlier. Jesus said, "Martha, trust me. The God who created the cosmos, whose love can overcome any obstacle, will restore your brother to life."

Jesus's words transformed their fear into confidence, and they rolled the stone away.

No one moved or spoke. The only sound was a gentle breeze rustling leaves on nearby trees. Hearts beat rapidly, and hands were clammy with eager anticipation of what would happen next.

Jesus' strong voice pierced the silence. "Lazarus, come out!"

Everyone gasped as Lazarus appeared, his limbs still bound with strips of cloth. They shrank back; was it safe to approach someone who had been in the grave? Wasn't he unclean? What would Jesus do now?

---

10. Both the NRSV footnote for verses 11:33-35 (pg. 1931), and the NIV Application Commentary (p. 318) note that the verb translated "disturbed" or "deeply moved" is better translated as agitation, indignation, outrage, fury, or anger.

11. From John 11:35. "Jesus' tears should be connected to the anger [over death] he is feeling so deeply." Gary M. Burge, The NIV Application Commentary: John, pg. 318.

12. John 11:34, NIV

13. John 11:38; See above note regarding the translation of "deeply moved" (NIV) or "greatly disturbed" (NRSV).

14. John 11:39, NIV

15. John 11:39, NIV

Jesus embraced his friend, tears of joy streaming down his face, alleviating their doubts. He turned to Martha and Mary and told them to remove the grave cloths, and they gratefully unwound the remaining evidence of their brother's suffering.

Lazarus gazed at Jesus, his sisters, and his friends. He could feel their love warming him and renewing his strength. The gift he received from Jesus was humbling; Lazarus felt overwhelmed with gratitude at being restored to life and love.

As Jesus prepared to leave with his disciples, Lazarus locked eyes with him. Tears welled up, and words caught in his throat. Jesus smiled and nodded, then turned toward Jerusalem; the next phase of his mission awaited.

Lazarus' Story Mirrors Our Inner Story

Lazarus represents the exiles in our internal family, the "sick" parts of us. They are wounded and bear the burdens of adversity.

When a loved one is struggling, other family members take action. Our protectors adopt roles to shield the system from the impact of an exile's wounds. In this story, Mary and Martha function like dedicated protectors. They are afraid and anxious, so they call for help. Similarly, our protectors alert us to the presence of an exile. Imagine the scene outside Mary and Martha's home as dozens of people gather to mourn Lazarus, wailing and crying.

Sometimes, the reactivity of our protectors feels similarly chaotic. Imagine being blindsided by unexpected criticism, setting off a chain reaction from exiles and protectors. Exiles who carry burdens from other times they were harshly criticized feel rejected or condemned. Their shame erupts, along with beliefs about being unlovable or abandoned. Then inner critics blast you for failing to meet someone's standard or for saying or doing something that led to being blindsided. A caretaking part might get into an argument with your critic, blaming the person who criticized you. It's all too much, so in comes a firefighter who has you grabbing a bottle of wine or eating a pint of ice cream.

Because protectors fear we will be overwhelmed by an exile's pain, they block connection with it. Jesus' disciples feared what would happen if he returned to Judea, and Martha feared opening the tomb would release the stench of decay. Jesus tried to shift their focus to a broader perspective—to keep them centered on the promise of healing. But, as with our protectors, they fixated on threats and had difficulty trusting that healing was possible.

Jesus reassured his disciples and Martha, but I can imagine a last line of resistance to embracing Lazarus: dead bodies were considered unclean. There are often layers of protectors surrounding our exiles. Jesus models patience and persistence, two vital qualities in interacting with protectors.

Given the many protective strategies at work within us, the Self must provide hope, reassurance, and courage. Ultimately, when they trust the Self, protectors will relax and allow access to exiles.

Lazarus emerged from the tomb, still bound by grave cloths. When the Self first connects with an exile, they hold burdens. They need assistance to become free from what binds them, and there are several steps in the process. After healing, they can return to their original state—to reclaim their life, as Lazarus reclaimed his.

The Web of Relationships—Self, Exiles, and Protectors

The remainder of this chapter casts a vision for the healing that is possible for your exiles. Dr. Schwartz consistently cautions against attempting to work with our exiles without the help of a trained IFS professional.[16] It is challenging to consistently detect the presence of protectors and unblend from them when exiles begin sharing their burdens. IFS therapists are "parts detectors;" we spend many hours sitting with clients and feeling the difference between Self, protectors, and exiles. I do not want you to feel frustrated or overwhelmed by prematurely trying to be with exiles.

Please read this section with hope for what is possible with proper support for your journey into the most tender territory of your inner world. Because it would be tedious to refer to "you and your therapist" repeatedly, I refer to your experience with your system. Still, I encourage you to remember the importance of being accompanied by a skilled guide in this phase of your healing journey.

Even with the support of an IFS professional, you will spend significant time with protectors before you have access to exiles. Cultivating relationships with

---

16. You can find an IFS therapist in your area through the IFS Institute website: https://ifs-institute.com/practitioners

your protectors, as you have begun doing through the practices following each chapter, prepares your internal family for the delicate work of supporting exiles in releasing their burdens.

Building trust with protectors takes as long as it takes. Some protectors will trust you more readily than others; some will trust you on Monday and will be full of doubt and fear by Thursday. The path you are traveling is not a straight line. It is a winding, boulder-strewn, uphill climb to a destination that sometimes seems like it is always just over the next ridge.

Trust develops as you spend time connecting with members of your inner family, patiently and persistently building relationships. Just as meaningful relationships with friends require time and effort, your commitment to turning toward protectors when you notice them builds trust and confidence in your leadership. When you offer attention and appreciation, they feel seen—one of their greatest desires.

More often than not, healing takes time simply because it takes time to cultivate relationships. The time you spend connecting with protectors is as important as connecting with exiles. Protectors are members of your internal family who have burdens of their own. Circumstances outside their control have hijacked their lives, and they need love just as much as exiles do.

With these caveats in mind, let's explore the healing steps used in IFS therapy so you have a road map for the most vulnerable terrain in your internal system.[17] Knowing the steps builds hope for healing, even though you need a guide to travel this tender territory. Parts of you will feel relieved as they learn that, while nuanced and sometimes complex, healing is not a mysterious unknown. This process is supported by research[18] and by the testimony of people worldwide who have benefitted from it. Given the power of the approach, it is not surprising that we see key biblical themes of redemption, restoration, and reconciliation.

---

17. *Internal Family Systems Therapy, 2nd ed.,* Richard C. Schwartz and Martha Sweezy, pg. 164

18. For example, see https://www.jrheum.org/content/jrheum/early/2013/08/10/jrheum.121465.full.pdf

The Healing Steps

Befriending. When protectors trust you, they will tell you what they fear will happen if they stop doing what they're doing. That is the doorway to your exiles. You will hear something related to the job they do. For example, "If I stop criticizing you, you will be shamed just like in first grade when your teacher shamed you." Or, "If I relax, you will be blindsided like you were when he betrayed you." Protectors will show you the scene where your exile lives. You must ask them for permission to connect with the exile when they do so. "Thank you for sharing your fears with me. I'm glad you trust me; I know it isn't easy. Would it be okay with you if I spent time with her? I can help her; she won't overwhelm the system with her pain."

When you are in direct contact with the exile, you befriend them. As you learned in previous chapters, befriending is simply using the relationship skills you already possess to connect with one of your internal family members. Typically, curiosity guides the interaction. Asking open-ended questions and paying attention to how the part responds to your presence builds your connection.

The nuance to be aware of with exiles is that they have been cut off from contact with you for what is often many, many years. If you approach them and they seem disinterested or afraid—and you have made sure your heart is open—they need time with you to trust your loving presence. Your presence can be more impactful than words. Imagine a sacred space that is safe, and invite them to join you. Be with them, allowing them to be just as they are without needing anything to happen. Notice how they respond to being with you. Their posture might change; they sometimes come closer to you or look you in the eyes. These are signals that they are beginning to be interested in connecting with you.

When you sense that they are aware of you and are open to connecting, let them know you care about them and their story, and invite them to share it with you.

Witnessing. The heart of the healing process is when the exile tells the Self about their experiences—when *they* share their story. You might be very familiar with their story; parts of you who are historians or storytellers have shared it often. But the part of you who experienced the events—the one who carries the pain and was cut off to protect you—hasn't told their story to *you*. They haven't felt unconditional love and acceptance because they've been surrounded by protectors working to keep them hidden. Therefore, you must allow the exile to tell their story at the pace that feels right to them.

An open-ended invitation such as, "I would like you to let me feel and see and sense what it is like for you," gives the exile your full attention and encourages them to communicate through emotions, images, and sensations.[19] Younger exiles often share sensations and emotions more than words or pictures.

It is important to accept whatever the exile offers as the meaning they made of the events they experienced. You can also ask, "What happened to make you feel [sad, angry, confused, abandoned]?"

Patience is a vital element of Self-energy for this stage of the healing process. Exiles often open up slowly. If you feel uncomfortable with their silence or doubt your ability to offer what they need, a protector has slipped back in. That often happens, and we ask them to step back. If they persist, you will want to find out why they changed their mind about letting you connect with the exile.

Some exiles will be upset with you. It's not unusual for them to say, "Where were you when I needed you?" An apology is vital; you weren't there in the way you are now. Tell them how sorry you are that they felt alone and unsupported. Reassure them that you are here now and want to help them heal.

Exiles have been cut off from the internal family because they hold intense emotions. Extending empathy—feeling *with* them—provides space for them to share their feelings freely.[20] Remember, protectors fear exiles' emotions will overwhelm you, so they have worked to contain them. Your wounded exiles need to know you can handle what they feel—and you, the Self who is the leader of the internal family—*can* handle it. In the presence of Self-energy, love flows, and the exile realizes they do not have to overwhelm you.

It can take time for exiles to trust the Self; they don't know you. If you turn toward them and they flood you with their distress, you can use your breath to create a sacred space for connection. Rather than using your breath to push them

---

19. Select phrases in this section are adapted from *No Bad Parts: Healing Trauma & Restoring Wholeness With the Internal Family Systems Model,* by Richard C. Schwartz, PhD, pgs.115-117

20. *Internal Family Systems Therapy, 2nd ed.,* Richard C. Schwartz and Martha Sweezy, pg. 160

away, the practice invites them to feel the flow of loving energy as you breathe deeply together and exhale slowly. Imagine breathing in grace and exhaling peace.

As details of the story emerge, parts of you might protest, saying, "That couldn't have happened." Others might be skeptical. Reassure them that listening to exiles is not detective work. It is not about gathering facts to build a case. You are offering the loving presence they lacked when something distressing happened. Healing does not rest on knowing what exactly happened. Exiles heal when we listen and validate the impact of their experiences. The *meaning they made* of events wounds them; what "actually happened" in objective reality is largely irrelevant to the healing process.

Exiles often hold distorted beliefs because they interpret events as their fault. If a parent is overly harsh or abusive, the child might believe, "I'm bad; I deserved it," or "I'm unlovable." Children can think they should have had the power to keep an adult alive or a marriage from ending. The Self can say, "I see it differently. You were a child, and it was not your responsibility to care for them, or you didn't have the power to control their choices, much as you wish you did." Notice the exile's response to a new perspective. The goal is not to convince them they are wrong but to offer another, better option for their consideration.

Witnessing an exile's story is not usually a one-time event. Stories unfold over many walks along the river or quiet times tucked into your favorite chair. While parts of us might want to rush the process, the Self is patient. Allowing exiles the freedom to share as they choose restores their sense of agency—something lost due to adversity.

Clients often ask whether the Self can grieve because sadness is a natural response to the stories exiles tell. When a group of friends mourning the death of Lazarus confronts Jesus, Scripture records that "Jesus wept."[21] Exiles have always experienced loss—loss of nurturing care, loss of safety, loss of self-efficacy, loss of their worth—so they carry grief. And in their presence, your soul grieves with them.

You might wonder if you should invite God, Jesus, or the Spirit to be present as the exile's story unfolds. Whether you explicitly ask or not, they are, in fact, already present. The Source of Love, Revealer of Love, and Presence of Love are

21. John 11:35, NIV

with you always.[22] However you imagine the Divine, God *is love.*[23] Love is the energy that binds all of creation together. It flows in the Trinity and reaches for each of us—all parts of us—inviting us into the flow.[24] Your exile might want to imagine something representing Love, or it might spontaneously appear. I have had that experience, and I cherish the image of Love that appeared in my system as a precious gift. I encourage you to allow whatever happens to unfold organically. You will be awed by the creative ways parts of you connect with God.

Witnessing is the step in the healing process where an exile who was left for dead, like Lazarus in the tomb, has the opportunity to be seen and known—our greatest need. Holding space for an exile to share their story is a sacred process that takes as long as it takes. Patiently asking, "What do you need?" or "How can I help you?" reinforces a new reality: they now have the supportive person they lacked when they were hurt.

When sorrow wells up, let them know how sorry you are that they suffered. You will know what to say because Love is flowing. Your heart is open, and you are resonating with this vulnerable part cut off from connection. They have been in a tomb behind a stone. Their protectors rolled the stone over the entrance because they believed they had no other choice, but now they trust you to help the exile. Protectors are witnessing along with you; they are the family who gathered near the tomb and welcomed Lazarus back into the community.

Do-Over. Many avoid delving into their past because they believe, "You can't change what happened, so why bother?" Indeed, you can't change historical facts. What can be changed, however, is the meaning parts made of what happened to them.

Imagination is one of the most potent resources God gives us. When we use it to help an exile do what they needed when adversity occurred, our brains heal. The neural pathways holding adversity are changed. Frank Anderson, a psychiatrist and expert in using IFS to heal complex trauma, writes, "When the Self can be with,

---

22. I am indebted to my pastor, Steven Koski, for this description of the triune God.

23. 1 John 4:8, NIV

24. *The Divine Dance: The Trinity and Your Transformation,* Richard Rohr with Mike Morrell, pg. 67

listen to, validate, and give the part what it needed, wanted, and never got" that "promotes the correcting, updating, and rewiring of the neural network" holding the experience.[25]

If an exile was young, there could be an adult they want the Self to speak to on their behalf. If they feel powerless, the Self could empower them to do what they could not do in the past. You ask, "What do you need? How can I help you?" With imagination, there are no limits to what you can do with or for them.

Exiles often carry anger and need support from you in expressing it. Anger is the emotional response to injustice, a common experience for exiles. They were demeaned, ignored, shamed, or abused. Of course they are angry! Expressing anger when events occurred might have been dangerous; it could have provoked punishment or abuse. Allowing them to express anger supports transformation. If protectors are nervous about this, that's a signal to slow down and spend time with them.

At every step of this process, it is vital to assess for Self-leadership. If you aren't leading the process with confidence, clarity, courage, compassion, creativity, calm, curiosity, and connection, that means that protectors have stepped back in. When Self leads in harmony with the Holy Spirit, you will also be aware of the fruit of the Spirit: love, joy, peace, patience, kindness, generosity, faithfulness, gentleness and self-control.[26] Any manifestation of love reflects the leadership of Self and Spirit.

Retrieval. Our exiles live in a time and place rife with pain. When they have shared their story and had the opportunity to craft an empowering and healing version, they are ready to leave the past and be in the present with you, or in any other place they feel free to be themselves.

Because it can take many visits with an exile for them to share their whole story, we can also offer them a place of respite—someplace they go where they feel safe before telling us more about what happened. You will be delighted by the creative solutions they come up with!

---

25. *Transcending Trauma: Healing Complex PTSD with Internal Family Systems Therapy,* Frank G. Anderson, pg. 182

26. Galatians 5:22, NRSV

Unburdening. Exiles might spontaneously release emotions and distorted beliefs as they share their story and deepen their connection with you. After they decide to leave the time and place where adverse events occurred, we invite them to release any additional burdens they are still holding—including emotions, sensations, images, beliefs, and impulses.

This step in the healing process is a ritual—an intentional, embodied, and relational act that marks a milestone. Trauma expert Bessel van der Kolk writes, "Since time immemorial human beings have used communal rituals to cope with their most powerful and terrifying feelings."[27] The community of Self, Spirit, and protectors holds space for the exile as they unload all they've carried since being wounded.

As we notice burdens, we ask, "Would you like to release it?" Exiles are often eager to release their pain but might need support; we encourage unloading the energy of their burdens to the powerful elements of creation—earth, air, fire, and water. The power of life is in each of the elements, transforming pain. Imagine a burden like a seed encased in a hard shell. Fire releases the seed from the cone, and the wind carries it to fertile earth, where water nourishes it. Exiles will often have a preferred element they use in their unburdening.

Sometimes, exiles release burdens to Jesus, the Light, or the Spirit. Creativity flows during the unburdening ritual; the power of imagination to transform pain is moving.

Like witnessing, unburdening might unfold over time. In the presence of Self and Spirit, exiles will feel empowered to choose what works best for them. This ritual marks a turning point in an exile's journey of healing.

Invitation. Exiles are restored to full membership in your internal family when they release burdens. They are ready to reclaim the qualities blocked by pain. We do not offer suggestions; they tell us what they want to recover. They know what was lost. They have gifts, and it's moving to be present with them as their vital qualities are restored. You might hear "C" qualities or the return of childlike spontaneity, wonder, and playfulness. Take your time with this step of the process. Join your exile in feeling each of the qualities in your body. Sometimes, you can do

---

27. *The Body Keeps the Score: Brain, Mind, and Body in the Healing of Trauma,* Bessel van der Kolk, pg. 331

an activity related to the quality together. I recall a client whose inner child wanted to ride her bike after unburdening; I know another who wanted to go on a long hike in the wilderness. Often, our inner children want to play or dance.

Integration. Integration is the theoretical term for wholeness—*shalom,* harmonious co-existence. It is the stage where you invite the whole internal family system to notice and respond to one member's healing. As you know, your exile is a member of a larger family. Their healing process does not happen in a vacuum; protectors watch it unfold. After exiles reclaim their gifts, the Self invites the rest of the inner family to respond to what occurred. Often, protectors are relieved; they can give up the jobs they've been doing because they are no longer necessary. That can happen spontaneously, or they might also need to experience the healing steps to unburden and reclaim their vital qualities.

Restoring Wholeness

The healing steps provide what burdened internal family members need to recover from adversity's impact. Telling their stories to a trusted witness enables them to regain their sense of self-efficacy and confidence in their worth. Releasing burdens creates space for essential qualities—the gifts they bring to the world. And when exiles heal, protectors are free to unload the burden of adaptive strategies adopted to survive. When one inner family member heals, there is a ripple effect throughout the system. Constraints to love in all of its forms are released. The system shifts from chaos and discord to harmony. Love flows freely—a state of *shalom.*

This process is a re-enactment of the metanarrative of Scripture. The vision for our lives in Genesis, where God declares all things "good," is echoed in the Great Commandment—love freely flowing to and from God, others, and ourselves. But the vision is marred by brokenness. In our broken state, we exile risky vulnerability. Exile is never the end of the story—for the enslaved Israelites in Egypt, the Judahites in Babylon, or the suffering people Jesus touched with healing. Exiles are reclaimed; their suffering is redeemed. The Spirit moves like the wind, bringing freedom and recovery to the oppressed.[28] Everyone is welcome at the banquet

28. From Luke 4:18-19

table to celebrate restoration and reconciliation. Now you can carry the vision inside, bringing Love to every part of you.

Loving ourselves is an essential practice—a vital element of the Great Commandment. The Great Commandment provides a vision of *shalom*; it places us in a web of reciprocal, loving relationships. As we love ourselves, we are freer to love God and others. Extending healing to our external relationships is the next step on our journey to *shalom.*

Spiritual Practice: Listening with Love

Perhaps you've already sensed what is often the case: exiles tend to be young. They are our "inner children," a term used in various psychological and spiritual texts. You can think of your connection with them as a process of re-parenting. You will be the ideal parent they deserved but did not have. While most parents do their best, none are perfect. There are inevitable ruptures in the parent-child relationship, some of which remain stuck in our system, burdening an exile.

One of the foremost parenting experts, Dr. Daniel Siegel, emphasizes the importance of "contingent communication," where "signals sent by the child are directly perceived, understood, and responded to by the parent in a dance of communication that involves mutual collaboration."[29]

Think of being with your exile in a sacred space of connection as an opportunity to perceive their experience, understand it, and respond to it by validating it and holding it with respect and gentleness. And they will have the chance to collaborate with you in their healing by sharing their experience, communicating their needs, and being supported in taking action.

---

29. *Parenting from the Inside Out: How a Deeper Self-Understanding Can Help You Raise Children Who Thrive,* Daniel J. Siegel and Mary Hartzell, pg. 81

When the Self meets an exile in a space where the Spirit flows freely, the exile will have the connection they need for feeling safe, seen, soothed, and secure.[30] They are safe because they are no longer alone, seen by the loving eyes of Self and Spirit, soothed by compassion, and secure as they trust you will always be with them.

If you feel calm and confident about connecting with an exile, the following practice will help you lead from Self as you invite a vulnerable member of your inner family to share their story. If connecting with an exile provokes protectors—you feel anxious, fearful, or distracted—please skip this practice.

- Find a picture of yourself as a child at the age when you experienced adversity. Notice what arises when you look at it. How do you feel toward them?
- No matter how confident you are that you are ready to connect with an exile, protectors can slip back in when a plan becomes a reality. If you aren't curious, compassionate, or confident, shift your attention to your protectors. Ask them if they would allow you to spend time with the child in the photo. If they do not relax, connect with them to learn more.
    - This might be as far as you can go alone, and that's okay! Building relationships with your protectors is always valuable.
- When you feel curious or compassionate as you look at the photo, let them know you are here to help and you'd like to spend time with them.
- Close your eyes now that you have their image in mind. Imagine being with them in a sacred space filled with the Spirit.
- How are they responding to your presence? Can you accept their response gracefully—allowing it to be just as it is, without needing it to change?
- If you sense they are hostile or disinterested, let them know you are sorry you couldn't be with them back then the way you can be with them now. Notice their response.

30. Ibid, pg. 108

- Just be with them, letting them feel your loving energy so they know they can trust they aren't alone.
- Notice if they are looking at you and how far away they are. Eye contact and proximity to them signal safety.
- You might already be getting information from them—emotions, words, images. If so, allow them to continue to share. Or, ask them, "Would you like to share anything with me?"
- Remember, it is your job to perceive (listen attentively), understand, and respond kindly to what they share. The most important of these, at least initially, is to listen.
    - If you want to reflect on what they share to demonstrate understanding, you can say, "It feels like you are sad (or scared or lonely)."
    - Respond in a way that's congruent with what they are sharing. For example, you can apologize for not being with them or tell them you are sorry for what they experienced, or validate that the way they responded was sensible given the circumstances.
- Consistent connection builds trust, and stories often unfold over several meetings. Can you commit to spending time with this vulnerable member of your inner family?
- Use your journal to note the important elements of the interaction: what they experienced, how you felt toward them, and how they responded to you.

Chapter Ten

My Story Connects Me to Yours

Luke 10:25-37

Ezra[1] was preoccupied as he navigated the rugged road from Jerusalem to Jericho. He wondered how the students of the Law received his teaching. Recalling the spark in their eyes and thoughtful questions, Ezra felt increasingly confident that his pupils revered him as an esteemed teacher. He felt the flush of pleasure at his stature among the priests gathered in Jerusalem.

His musings were interrupted when he saw what appeared to be a man lying by the road. The sun was low, so he wasn't sure what he was seeing. Could it be someone lying in wait to rob him? Drawing closer, he realized the robbery had already been carried out. Laying by the roadside, bloodied and barely conscious, was a young man with his bags and belongings tattered and strewn about him.

Ezra thought, "I don't have time for this! Everyone is waiting for me to arrive home." He quickly crossed the road and picked up his pace, eager to join the festive family gathering celebrating his son's birthday.

Anxiety made Judah's heart pound. He hated walking home at dusk along this perilous road. Just last week, bandits robbed his friend. He would rather stay in his hometown than travel to Jerusalem just to be treated like a servant by the priests.

Judah resented the senior priests who took all the glory while he and the other Levites did the grunt work.[2] After all, his ancestors were Levites who faithfully

---

1. Ezra, Judah, and Benyamin are my fictional names for the men in this parable.

2. Priests were the primary teachers of the law, assisted by Levites. See *The New Testament in its World,* N.T. Wright & Michael F. Bird, pg. 128

served the Lord. He was proud of his heritage even if he wasn't a direct descendant of Aaron.[3]

The glow of pride dissipated when Judah noticed the hunched form of a man by the side of the road. Just as he feared, there must be bandits nearby! He felt a jolt of panic; he needed to get as far away from the man as possible. He could be bait! Judah ran to the other side of the road, feverishly scanning his surroundings for potential threats. His only concern was to get home safely.

Benyamin was tired after a stressful day doing business in Jerusalem.[4] He wished he could avoid going there; so many people treated him with disdain or contempt. One man even spat when he brushed his shoulder on a crowded street! His heart felt heavy as he grieved the impact of longstanding hatred between Jews and Samaritans. He was looking forward to soothing his nerves with a hot meal and a good night's sleep at the inn, one of his favorites.

Always alert for danger on the notoriously treacherous trip to Jericho, Benyamin noticed a dark shape by the side of the road. He cautiously approached, and found a young man lying there.

Benyamin quickly realized robbers had attacked him. He was bleeding and naked! Moved by compassion, Benyamin knelt and reassured the man that he would help him. He poured wine and oil on the wounds to clean and soothe them, then wrapped them tightly. Because the man was barely conscious, he gently helped him up on his donkey and set out for the inn.

Benyamin stayed awake to monitor the man's condition, offering him water and broth and a cool rag for his head. As dawn broke, the man slept peacefully and had not developed a fever, so Benyamin felt he could leave him in the innkeeper's care. He paid for the room and assured the innkeeper he would cover any additional costs when he returned.

As Benyamin rode toward Samaria, he prayed for the man's healing.

---

3. Levites were "lesser priests, male members of the tribe of Levi...while a 'priest' was a Levite descended from Aaron." *The New International Commentary on the New Testament: The Gospel of Luke,* Joel B. Green, pg. 64

4. Because he possessed a donkey, money, oil, and wine and Jerusalem held no religious significance, it is likely he represented a traveling merchant. *The New International Commentary on the New Testament: The Gospel of Luke,* Joel B. Green, pg. 431

Love Your Neighbor as You Love Yourself

On one of many occasions where religious authorities tested Jesus, an expert in the law asked him what he needed to do to inherit eternal life. Jesus didn't take the bait; he asked the expert, "What is written in the Law?"[5] The man answered, "'Love the Lord your God with all your heart and with all your soul and with all your strength and with all your mind,' and 'Love your neighbor as yourself.'"[6] "'Good answer!' said Jesus. 'Do it and you'll live.'"[7]

But the expert in the law didn't want to love without constraints, so he asked, "Who is my neighbor?"[8] One commentator suggests he asked the question "not so much to determine to whom he must show love, but...to calculate the identity of those to whom he need not show love."[9]

Can you relate to wanting some wiggle room? I can. Jesus draws a straight line between what God asks of us and our response, but it would be much more comfortable if the line went around some of the people we would rather ignore or avoid.

There is no grey in this narrative, however. Jesus asked the expert in the law which of the three men in the story was a neighbor to the wounded man. He answered, "The one who had mercy on him;" Jesus said, "Go and do likewise."[10]

Because living in the flow of love between ourselves, others, and God is essential for life, Jesus tells a story that, unlike many of his parables, is crystal clear. He wants us to understand what blocks the free flow of love, and he wants us to do something about it.

---

5. Luke 10:26, NIV

6. Luke 10:27, NIV

7. Luke 10:28, The Message

8. Luke 10:29, NIV

9. The New International Commentary on the New Testament: The Gospel of Luke, Joel B. Green, pg. 426

10. Luke 10:36-37, NIV

What happens inside of us when we face vulnerability? Is our heart open, or is it closed? Does compassion inspire action, or do protectors create barriers and make excuses? These are the questions the parable provokes. Digging into the details helps answer them and leads us to a practice that restores the flow of love inside and out.

Who is the Wounded Person?

Jesus is quite specific about the identity of the men who do—and do not—help the person who was "attacked by robbers," stripped, beaten, and left "half-dead."[11] A priest, a Levite, and a Samaritan each interact with him.

But what about the identity of the wounded man? We only know he was traveling from Jerusalem to Jericho. His clothes, which could have provided some identifying details, were gone. We do not know his nationality or religious affiliation. Commentators agree that his anonymity is purposeful.[12] Jesus teaches us he was a human being needing help, period.

In this story, Jesus paints a vivid picture of vulnerability. A group of robbers attacked a man traveling alone. Presumably, they were armed, but even if they weren't, there were at least two of them and only one traveler, so they had the power. They took his valuables, beat him until he was "half dead," and stripped him naked—inflicting the pain of shame. Alone, naked, weak, and in physical and emotional pain, the stranger is an exile. He desperately needed a loving connection with others to begin healing, as do all exiles—inside and out.

Protectors React to Vulnerability

The Parable of the Good Samaritan externalizes the dynamics we've been exploring in our internal family. The vulnerability of our wounded exiles provokes various protective reactions—like those of the priest and Levite—all of which block connection when it's most needed.

---

11. Luke 10:30, NIV

12. See The New Interpreter's Study Bible: NRSV note pg. 1874, and *The New International Commentary on the New Testament: The Gospel of Luke,* Joel B. Green, pg. 429

I imagine the Levite having one of the most common protective reactions: hypervigilance—always being on guard to detect possible threats. The road from Jerusalem to Jericho was known for being dangerous. It ran through "very rugged desert and wilderness terrain...with robbers regularly hiding out and preying on vulnerable individuals who weren't part of a larger caravan of travelers."[13] In an objectively threatening situation, the Levite was too preoccupied with his own safety to consider the other person's needs. His focus narrowed to his well-being, leaving no space for mercy.

The point is not to disregard personal safety, no matter the cost. But our protectors have only a partial perspective; their strategies are rooted in past experiences. They need our help—leadership from the Self—to determine present risk. The Samaritan stopped to help his fellow traveler and suffered no harm himself. He even stayed long enough to care for the man's wounds before taking him to the inn. Our protectors might say it's too dangerous to slow down, but our ultimate decision should rest on more than just their narrow view.

The priest's protective reaction is illuminated by research done at Princeton Seminary in the 1970s.[14] Researchers gave participants various instructions about a class assignment. They instructed half of the participants to give a talk about careers in ministry and told the other half to explain the Parable of the Good Samaritan. Then the groups were each broken into three subgroups and given varying amounts of time to prepare—from a few minutes to no time at all. Participants would share their presentations at a location across campus on a bitterly cold winter day. To get there, they passed by an alley where a man who was not adequately dressed for the weather was slumped over, coughing.

What do you think happened? Do you hope they all stopped to help—or at least those asked to share about the Parable of the Good Samaritan?

The study's outcome showed a correlation between people in the greatest hurry and not offering *any* kind of help.

Our culture values hurry. The faster we go or the busier we are, the more important we are. Conversations are clipped and superficial. "How are you?" doesn't really mean the person wants to know the details. Our reflexive response

---

13. *Preaching the Parables: From Responsible Interpretation to Powerful Proclamation,* Craig L. Blomberg, pg. 59

14. Ibid, pg. 57-58

is, "Fine!" even when we're anxious, depressed, or lonely. Needs—even blatant ones—are bypassed, dismissed, or minimized. It's too inconvenient to pay attention.

Concerns about our safety or preoccupation with our priorities are two of countless protective reactions that prompt us to "cross the road" rather than connect with someone in need. Because our protectors adopted their strategy to cope with our wounds, my response to vulnerability might look very different than yours. However, the question, "Who is my neighbor?" reveals a ubiquitous protective strategy.

All humans define others—by race, gender, ethnicity, sexual orientation, socioeconomic status, age, ability, education, size, and numerous other categories—as a way to assess status. Who has power? Power feels safe to protectors, while weakness feels shameful. Who is an insider? Categories define whether we are in or out. Being on the inside feels safe while being an outsider is threatening.

Underneath the categories lies the real question: Is this person *worthy* of my time and attention? Do they *deserve* compassion?

Jesus told the Parable of the Good Samaritan in a context fractured by religious, political, and cultural differences.[15] People huddled with their clans and viewed others with suspicion or disdain. As I write this, I am struck by how little has changed.

In this parable and throughout his ministry, Jesus blew through barriers to spread the radical message that God's kingdom welcomes and values everyone *equally.* To be a force of change in our fractured world, we must move beyond protective reactions to reach across divides with love.

Leading with Love

How can we approach others with mercy and compassion—with curiosity and a desire to connect—rather than fear, judgment, disdain, or pity?

My first job was in banking after graduating from college with an economics degree. During the training program, we spent time in every department, and I

15. *The New International Commentary on the New Testament: The Gospel of Luke,* Joel B. Green, pg. 429

have always remembered how they train tellers to spot counterfeit currency. They learn everything about real money—the paper's feel, the ink's colors, etc. When you are an expert in the real thing, it is easy to spot a fake. Cultivating awareness of the presence of Self and Spirit is one of the best ways to know when protectors surface.

When you have access to healing resources—the eight Cs of curiosity, compassion, connection, creativity, calm, confidence, clarity, and courage—your Self is leading the inner family in harmony with the Holy Spirit.

As Eugene Peterson describes the fruit of the Spirit in *The Message*, "When we live God's way," we feel "affection for others, exuberance about life, serenity. We develop a willingness to stick with things, a sense of compassion, and a conviction that a basic holiness permeates things and people. We find ourselves involved in loyal commitments, not needing to force our way in life, able to marshal and direct our energies wisely."[16]

You will notice the difference in your body when Self and Spirit lead. Your energy is calm and expansive rather than activated and anxious. Muscles are relaxed, not tense, and breathing is deep rather than shallow. Just as you can assess for qualities of Love, you can also scan your body to determine whether Love is leading your inner family.

As we meditate on the qualities of Love and become increasingly familiar with Love's presence, we more readily notice its absence. Love feels "absent" because it is blocked or constrained by our pain and the protective strategies pain provokes.

Love is always there; it cannot be obliterated by our exiles' burdens or the jobs protectors adopt. But if distress wells up and floods the system, we feel emotions like grief, panic, or shame instead of love. As you know, protectors fear we will be overwhelmed, so they take over to regain control. When protectors dominate, love is constrained, and our reaction to others shifts from curiosity and kindness to judgment and distance.

Making a You-Turn

To restore the inner family's Self-and-Spirit-leadership, we must cultivate awareness of our protectors and practice connecting with them. Dr. Schwartz calls

16. *The Message,* Eugene Peterson, Galatians 5:22-23

this making a "you-turn." When we are irritated or upset by someone, we tend to focus on their behavior, how they should change, etc. But, as we all know, that does not lead to change; it's disempowering and futile. If we shift our attention from the person who provoked a protective response back to ourselves and offer curiosity to members of our internal family, we can learn what's prompting our reactivity. As we unblend from protectors, we gain clarity about relationship issues and unlock the courage to address them.

The key is to practice being "parts detectors," able to notice sometimes subtle shifts in our inner system that signal a protector is present. The more familiar you are with protective strategies, the more likely you will be to catch the shift from being Self-led to protector-led so you can practice making a you-turn.

I am often asked, "Are protectors bad?" My answer is an emphatic *no.* They are invaluable members of the internal family. They alert us to risks, help us discern our needs, and lead us to the exiles who need healing. Our goal is to engage with them so we can glean vital information. However, because their perspective is narrower, we do not function as well when they lead the inner family; that is why the core of our practice is to build and maintain relationships with them. When they know and trust the Self, they will provide their information without needing to dominate our system. Ultimately, as exiles release burdens, our protectors will give up fear-driven roles but remain crucial team members. For example, a rigidly perfectionistic protector might become a helpful team member who offers the skill of organization. Remember, multiplicity is God's intended design for humans, and it is not the goal to lose the richness of our diverse parts.

As you know, protectors are creative and adopt myriad strategies. Some strategies are particularly evident in interpersonal relationships: judgment and boundary violations. Sometimes we will react to others with judgment or by violating their boundaries, and at other times we will be on the receiving end of these strategies. When we feel judged, or someone violates our boundaries, parts of us will react. Defensiveness or anger will dominate, blocking our desire to connect with the other person. If we are going to be able to reach across divides to connect with our neighbors—whether they are people in our community or our family—we must cultivate relationships with the parts of us who constrain God-given resources such as curiosity and compassion.

Judging the "Other"

The Parable of the Good Samaritan is shocking because religious leaders who, presumably, would be merciful according to their laws ignored the wounded man. They judged him unworthy of their compassion. Unfortunately, this still characterizes some contemporary Christian communities, where we talk about love but often fail to be loving, reacting with fear or shame-based strategies that build walls rather than bridges.

Why would a community that follows a God who "is love," a community instructed to "love each other deeply" and exhorted to patiently bear "with one another in love," opt for judgment instead of love?[17] What is powerful enough to push out the love that testifies to the profound mystery of God dwelling within each of us?

Fear. Fear of vulnerability motivates protective strategies, including judgment.

It is uncomfortable to explore judgment—particularly as a strategy one of *my* protectors employs. So this is a warning; this will not be the easiest part of this book. I have no doubt you will cringe reading about how we judge others. My point in exploring the topic from the perspective of being the one who judges is not to negate your experience of being on the receiving end of this pernicious protective impulse. It feels awful, and it significantly disrupts our inner family. Recovering from judgment takes intentional work with protectors and wounded exiles. Yet, when we practice making a you-turn to be with the least attractive parts of ourselves, we take a vital step in the work of real and lasting change.

Deep breath in; long exhale out. Let's dive in.

Judgment distances us from another person's challenges and blames—or shames—them for their circumstances. We elevate ourselves—which feels powerful to our protectors—when we decide a person deserves what happened because of poor choices or not following rules.

American culture is highly individualistic, and none of us are impervious to the influence of this ethos. The complex context in which each individual develops—with variable degrees of healthy attachment to caregivers, access to

17. 1 John 4:8, 1 Peter 4:8, Ephesians 4:2, NIV

resources, and support for flourishing—is lost when we focus solely on individual responsibility.

Instead of being curious about someone's story, we decide their symptoms—addiction, unstable relationships, illness, etc.—tell us all we need to know.

When we refer to someone—or ourselves—by a diagnosis or condition, we reduce the rich tapestry of our personhood and life to our greatest challenge. I cringe when I hear, "He's schizophrenic," or "She's bipolar," "I am an addict," or "She's a narcissist," or "He's a perpetrator."

Can you feel the protective energy in these reductionistic descriptions? If you're unsure, consider whether they build bridges or walls. When a part of you narrows your focus to one aspect of a person's identity, does your heart open or close? When you hear yourself label someone—and we all do it—you can make a you-turn to connect with the protector and learn what they fear would happen if you lead with love.

For over a decade, my daughter has worked in forensic social work as part of a team including public defenders. One of her roles is to dig into the history of a client charged with a crime to determine whether mitigating factors are relevant to their defense. For example, trauma, mental illness, and brain injury impact the appropriate consequences for the crimes. Her clients are "perpetrators" who are also human beings with complex and, often, tragic stories. They must bear the consequences of their actions, but they deserve more than judgment; Jesus says they, too, are our neighbors.

Have you been the victim of a crime? Do you wonder if this story means you must be a "neighbor" to the person who inflicted harm? *You* get to decide how—if at all—you engage with them. When responding to someone who is objectively unsafe, identifying and unblending from our natural—and vital—protective responses yields clarity, confidence, and courage. Led by Self and Spirit, you can respond in ways that respect your integrity and worth, including distancing yourself from harm. The more Self-led you are, the more you will be able to discern the best course of action. I do not think Jesus meant to teach that we are equally neighborly with every person in our lives; it's essential not to go beyond the text in ways that risk harm. The point of doing a you-turn to spend time with internal family members is to lead with love rather than judgment—and it can be loving to release someone to God who is not our responsibility.

Judgment is ubiquitous because it is intertwined with a primitive instinct to identify a core source of safety: being an insider. Imagine a group huddled together, pointing to someone and labeling them by race, size, ability, political preference, religion, etc. Our instinctive tendency to identify whether someone is "like us," an "insider," or "not like us," an "outsider," narrows our perspective. It is a protective strategy constraining a more expansive, loving mindset.

Unconscious biases—social stereotypes about certain groups of people held outside of conscious awareness—influence our view of others. Neuroscience shows that "the mere fact that the person is coded as *not like us*...results in differential treatment, with those *like-us* being treated better."[18] The greater our bias, the less likely our mirror neurons—neurons that promote empathy—are activated. When, through implicit bias, our brains automatically assign a person to a group we have coded as 'other,' we have less interest and empathy for that person.

The impulse to group people into "insiders" and "outsiders" is a primitive protective instinct we all share. As soon as our protectors categorize someone as "other" by labeling them, we are much less likely to see them as neighbors.

The illness or life circumstance, the worst thing we ever did, or the adaptive strategy we relied on for survival is not the most important thing about us. The most important thing is that we are Beloved. We are worthy of love—of being each other's neighbor. Reductionistic descriptions cast people out of the community, dehumanizing and disconnecting them from loving support. Jesus doesn't excuse this tendency because it's normative; he challenges us to do better.

As with so many things, Jesus flipped the script on labels when he invited marginalized people—"sinners"—to the table in God's kingdom. Throughout the Sermon on the Mount, Jesus upends our understanding of insiders and outsiders and vividly depicts how love flows in the kingdom. He repeats the phrase, "You have heard that it was said...But I tell you..." as he shifts from rigid, shaming rules to expansive grace.[19] The most striking statement—perhaps alarming to parts of us—is, "You have heard that it was said, 'Love your neighbor and hate your enemy.' But I tell you: Love your enemies and pray for those who persecute you."[20] Is this

18. https://nccc.georgetown.edu/bias/module-3/4.php

19. See Matthew 5:21-22, 27-28, 31-32, 33-34, 38-39, 43-44, NIV

20. Matthew 5:43-44, NIV

an impossible-to-live-out, hyperbolic teaching? I don't think so. Jesus knew love could give us new eyes to see beyond the superficial label "enemy" to the soul of another person equally loved by God.

In our polarized context, this is as difficult as ever. It's helpful to remember Jesus' context was equally polarized. Our only hope for transformation is to practice detecting protective energy in ourselves faithfully. As we consistently make a you-turn and unblend from protectors, we will have compassion for others whose protectors have hijacked their internal family. When we label someone, we can ask ourselves whether the label helps us identify vulnerability and need or whether it is a protective strategy to create distance. Our unconscious biases can become conscious as we make a you-turn and engage with protectors.

Navigating Boundaries

In contrast to using judgment to distance themselves from pain, some protectors do the opposite, violating boundaries through intrusive protective reactions. You might feel you are being neighborly when you offer advice or share a verse that challenges negative beliefs. These well-intentioned reactions are not as jarring as judgment or shaming, but they still reflect protective energy if offered without first asking, "What do you need?"

If, instead of listening with curiosity and compassion, we react with words that a suffering person hears as "You can't handle my pain; you aren't safe enough for my vulnerability," we shut the door of connection, leaving them alone with their distress. When we are alert to how our interaction is received—do our questions prompt dialog or does the person shut down and turn away?—we will know whether we are leading with Self and Spirit or if protectors uncomfortable with a person's vulnerability took over.

Have you been the person lovingly responding to needs—intentionally striking a balance between what's yours to do and what belongs to someone else—and being asked to do more? This is the flip side of intruding on someone else's boundaries; your boundaries were violated. You set a limit, then find yourself rationalizing why it's okay to disregard it, even though you feel bitter, irritated, or overwhelmed. Maybe you are afraid that saying no is risky; you'll pay the price for disappointing someone—perhaps losing status as an "insider" or invaluable team member. Or, you feel setting a boundary and sticking to it will end your relationship.

These problematic situations provoke many parts. They can trigger exiles holding painful experiences of being abandoned or excluded. Protectors, alert to their pain, can double down, ignoring the parts of you who are angry because of boundary violations. You will feel the tug-and-pull inside between warring factions who are alternately worried about how someone perceives you and irritated that they asked you to do more than your share. To arrive at sustainable decisions about what is yours to do, you must spend time with these activated members of your internal family.

Navigating boundaries is most challenging in our closest relationships because there is more at stake; it's more vulnerable when someone we love struggles. One of the most helpful assessment questions we can ask ourselves is, "Am I doing something for someone that they can and should do for themselves?"

We won't manage boundaries perfectly, but we can shift from anxious fretting that prompts boundary violations to Self-led clarity and patience that gives others space to discover their strengths. And we will learn to respect the information our protectors provide about times when people ask us to do more than is ours to do—or when a part of us believes that's the case.

My husband had an unusual situation: he knew his retirement date—from 35 years at the same job—four years in advance. I spent the first two years worried about how he would navigate the transition; I recall many conversations where I offered various options to prepare him. I suggested things he could get involved with beforehand, and we talked about him working remotely to shift his routine. It might not surprise you that I also convinced him to go to a couple of therapy workshops!

My advice was motivated by fear about his well-being—and mine. I was irritated by his lack of response to my ideas, and there was a consistent voice in my head blaming him for not doing anything to alter a long-standing routine. Thankfully, during that season, I did a deep dive into IFS. During an advanced training led by Dr. Schwartz, I participated in a demo—a live therapy session with Dr. Schwartz—in front of the group. We worked with the protector who thought it was her job to caretake my husband and discovered the exile who was stuck at a time early in our marriage when he was struggling to get started with his career. We went through the healing steps with her, and she unloaded her burdens. When we turned our attention back to the protector working hard to find solutions for my husband and asked her what her response was to seeing the young woman who was now free of her pain, she said, "Must be nice for her!" It was such a great reminder that our protectors are burdened too. Protectors do their jobs because they don't feel they have a choice, not because they enjoy it. So we supported her in unloading things that constrained her, freeing her up to contribute in another way. From that point, I have been able to be a resource during his ongoing transition without feeling responsible for it.

Balancing the ever-changing nuances of responsibility versus support is one of the most significant parental challenges. Raising children is a constant process of evaluating shifting developmental needs and how that affects the nature of parenting.[21] Parents *will* cross the line and do things for a child that they can and should do for themselves. The key is to catch ourselves and recognize when a well-intentioned protector is leading with worry or a desire for control rather than Self-led clarity and confidence about the child's capabilities. As a parent of children in their 30s, I can testify that we must always be alert for sometimes subtle boundary violations.

Similar dilemmas arise if we are in a supportive role for aging parents. Am I hovering and disrespecting an elder's agency because of my fear and grief? I spent four years as a counselor at a hospice, and one of the most impactful things I learned was how aging is a gradual process of losing control, particularly as we near death. It is a complex process for everyone in the family, and it inevitably provokes parts of us who react to upwelling waves of emotion. As you know, protectors fear we will be overwhelmed—and they can project that onto others. Rather than jumping in to caretake or give advice, when we make a you-turn and help protectors relax, we can offer space for others to express needs and process the impact of their experience. We can support our elders in asserting their agency and living from their strengths.

While protectors mean well, even caretakers who rush in to ease someone's pain can block loving connection when it's most needed. Rather than criticizing ourselves for a reaction that violates boundaries, we can turn toward our protectors to cultivate a trusting relationship. Making a you-turn shifts our focus inside. With curiosity, we connect with whoever is present to learn more about why they are there.

---

21. For parenting support, I recommend Daniel Siegel's many excellent books.

Protectors are on the job because of *your* story; they are connected to *your* exiles. A particular type of vulnerability—loss, betrayal, illness—might be kryptonite for our protectors but not for someone else's. Our protectors don't know that; when confronted by vulnerability, they react because they fear it will trigger exiles or because it already has. Their activity is a clue someone in your internal family needs attention. Practicing the you-turn helps us love all parts of ourselves so we can love our neighbors.

The Great Commandment is a Vision of Shalom

Most of the time, when I hear someone paraphrase the Great Commandment, they say, "Love God and others," leaving out "as we love ourselves." In some Christian spaces, there's an allergic reaction to loving ourselves. Verses are plucked out of context and used to teach us—particularly women—to ignore our needs. Serving others is distorted into the false command to "serve others at the expense of yourself."

Nothing in God's creation survives—let alone thrives—if needs are unmet. Despite the ubiquitous crowds of desperate people surrounding Jesus, he frequently withdrew to meet his greatest need: connection with God. We cannot meet others' needs if we neglect our own. And one of our greatest needs is to cultivate relationships with our internal family members to energize our lives with "living water."[22] Through building relationships with them, we restore parts cut off from God's love to the inner family. Transforming our internal chaos or rigidity into an integrated and flowing whole allows us to approach others with a desire to cultivate wholeness in all of our relationships. Instead of protecting scarce resources, an inexhaustible source of love energizes us.

When our hearts are blocked and love is constrained, we lose connection with ourselves, others, and God. Clarity about how best to respond to another person's needs is lost, and we are likely to distance ourselves or overfunction—doing more for someone than is healthy for them and us. Boundaries are rigid or porous rather than flexible and appropriate for the situation.

As we practice making a you-turn and lovingly connect with all parts of ourselves, we are much more likely to approach other people with curiosity and the

---

22. John 4:10, NIV

understanding that what we see on the surface is not the whole story. Protectors who would otherwise label others as a way to avoid vulnerability and maintain control begin to loosen their grip, releasing the constraints on our God-given resources.

With more access to healing resources, we are open to others' needs and have greater clarity about our role in meeting them. The Samaritan helped the man, *and* he involved the innkeeper in his care. The alternative to "crossing the street" is not taking sole responsibility when that is not appropriate. We have differing responsibilities and boundaries in various relationships. Wisdom and love guide our response when the Self leads the internal family.

Ultimately, as we practice loving all parts of ourselves—freeing exiles from their burdens and protectors from roles that constrain their best qualities—fear dissipates, and love flows freely, nourishing relationships inside and out. Curiosity replaces caution in interpersonal relationships as we trust God's invitation to see others as God sees them.

Dr. Curt Thompson says, "We are all looking for someone looking for us."[23] What feels better than looking into eyes that see you as you are and love you unconditionally? Equally impactful is offering those loving eyes to someone in need. This is *shalom*—relationships redeemed and reconciled, whole and free.

Spiritual Practice: Connecting with Parts Who React to Others

When we notice parts of us reluctant to see someone as our "neighbor," practicing the "you-turn" facilitates a return to Self-leadership. These questions shift your attention from external situations and people to your inner family. As you ask yourself these questions, you will identify different parts of yourself. Note them, and consider using the steps in previous chapters to connect with them.

---

23. Quoted in Tish Harrison Warren's opinion piece: https://www.nytimes.com/2023/06/04/opinion/relationships-digital-life.html

- How do I react when I'm unsure of how to respond?
- What situations or emotions do I avoid?
- When do I rush to resolve something rather than allow it to be as it is?
- What happens inside when I see someone in need?
- What label (political, religious, identity, sexual preference, etc.) provokes parts of me?

Imagine yourself on the road from Jerusalem to Jericho. It's hot and dusty; you're thirsty, and your feet are sore. Your mind is preoccupied with your concerns—a transition you're navigating, a troublesome relationship, or stressful demands on your time. The comforts of home beckon, but you notice someone in need. The person is someone you are biased against—be specific when you imagine them: age, race, gender, life circumstances, personality. What is your response? Who among your protectors perks up to convince you they are not your neighbor? Spend time with whoever you notice inside.

Chapter Eleven

Your Sacred Story

1 Corinthians 12:15-13:13

Chloe was eager to hear the Apostle Paul's letter.[1] The unity and grace characterizing their early months as a fledgling band of Jesus followers had given way to infighting and selfishness. Her hope for healing and harmony in her and others' lives was waning. She wondered if the Spirit was powerfully present in each of them, as promised. Chloe was weary of the debates in the community and within herself.

As she and others from her household gathered for the reading, Chloe could feel the tension. Some were already mumbling about whether they should listen to Paul rather than Apollos or Cephas.[2] Part of her feared a heated argument would erupt before Stephanus could read the letter. Her heart pounded, and her stomach clenched with anxiety.

Stephanus stood up and opened the letter. Chloe was distracted by a part of her who was watching for signs of hostility until the words "grace and peace to you from the Lord Jesus Christ"[3] penetrated her anxious fog. Those familiar words eased her concerns and helped her focus.

As Stephanus read, Chloe was struck by how diligently and faithfully Paul addressed the concerns shared with him. Some of his responses provoked discussion, but there were no heated arguments.

---

1. Members of Chloe's household informed Paul of problems in the Corinthian church. NIV Study Bible, pg. 1999. See also 1 Corinthians 1:11

2. 1 Corinthians 1:12, NIV

3. 1 Corinthians 1:3, NIV

Chloe listened even more attentively when Stephanus read, "Now about the gifts of the Spirit, brothers and sisters, I do not want you to be uninformed."[4] Her confusion over the power and presence of the Spirit was distressing. When she first heard Paul's message about Jesus, she *felt* the Spirit's power begin to heal her. She saw the effect it had on others and understood that, somehow, the Spirit was the loving energy of the Creator God living in and among them. Then people started arguing about the evidence of the Spirit in their lives and whether simple acts of service were as important as teaching and leading. Gradually, the loving connection they shared eroded.

Paul's words spoke directly to her heart. "God's various gifts are handed out everywhere, but they all originate in God's Spirit. God's various ministries are carried out everywhere, but they all originate in God's Spirit. God's various expressions of power are in action everywhere, but God is behind it all...All kinds of things are handed out by the Spirit, and to all kinds of people!"[5]

Chloe's shoulders relaxed, the tension in her gut eased, and her breathing deepened with the reassurance that the Spirit flowed freely, empowering and equipping all of them. Surely this teaching would resolve some of the conflicts!

Eager for more teaching to restore her confidence, Chloe carefully listened as Stephanus read, "Just as a body, though one, has many parts, but all its many parts form one body," so it is with Jesus-followers empowered by the Spirit. Whatever your previous religion or status, you are one body with many equally valuable parts.[6] Unity is what Chloe loved about their community! People who would never have considered each other friends and neighbors banded together to live with generosity and concern for one another.

As Stephanus continued, Chloe chuckled at Paul's clever way of highlighting the futility of debates over power and privilege. A foot feeling it didn't belong because it wasn't a hand, and an ear wishing it were an eye![7]

When he read, "Those parts of the body that seem to be weaker are indispensable, and the parts that we think are less honorable we treat with special

---

4. 1 Corinthians 12:1, NIV

5. 1 Corinthians 12:4-6, The Message, Eugene Peterson

6. 1 Corinthians 12:12-14, NIV and paraphrase

7. 1 Corinthians 12:15-17

honor,"[8] Chloe felt tears of relief well up. It was as though the Spirit were speaking to the tender, vulnerable parts of her who felt unlovable and unworthy. She was aware of all the strategies she used to hide them—taking care of others to earn approval, criticizing herself for flaws before someone else could, and distracting herself with busyness. Exhaustion was the price she paid, but she didn't feel she had a choice.

Paul's letter reminded her of the message that captivated her the first time she heard it: God gives the greatest honor to the parts of us who are bereft and most in need of loving-kindness. Jesus focused on the exiles and the marginalized—those deemed weak or disreputable. For the first time, Chloe realized that what was true for the community was also true for all parts of *her*. God valued everything about her! When Stephanus read, "There should be no division in the body, but...its parts should have equal concern for each other,"[9] she felt the Spirit give her a vision for how she should love herself.

She thought for a moment that she'd blurted out her epiphany to the whole group when she heard, "And yet I will show you the most excellent way."[10] Yes! This new vision of a diverse yet harmonious and supportive community *inside and out* was the message Jesus shared. This is what it means to live in God's kingdom now—to love God, others, and ourselves.

Tears flowed as Stephanus continued reading; Chloe felt the Spirit expanding her vision of love. "Love is patient; love is kind; love is not envious or boastful or arrogant or rude. It does not insist on its own way; it is not irritable or resentful; it does not rejoice in wrongdoing, but rejoices in the truth. It always protects, always trusts, always hopes, always perseveres. Love never fails."[11]

Love never fails. Chloe was energized by the confidence that nothing was beyond the reach of God's love. Her pain, and her efforts to cope with it, were held by parts of her *honored* by God. Rather than hiding under the protective layer of busyness and caretaking, Chloe felt God saying, "I see you, I love you, and I want to restore you to wholeness."

---

8. 1 Corinthians 12:22-23, NIV

9. 1 Corinthians 12:25, NIV

10. 1 Corinthians 12:31, NIV

11. 1 Corinthians 13:4-8; NRSV except v. 7, NIV

Chloe lifted her head and met the eyes of others as the words "Love never fails" reverberated through the room. She still felt the weight of the struggles and challenges within herself and among her friends, but rather than being flooded with fear and uncertainty, she felt hopeful. Calm and confidence welled up; with God's reconciling love for themselves and others, they could live out the promise of *shalom.*

What Kind of Love Is This?

How can we trust that love never fails? In human relationships, love can be precarious, and it can seem to fail. To lean into the promise that love never fails, we must understand the love to which Paul refers. It is not an emotion; it is the life force sustaining creation.

Richard Rohr writes, "The energy in the universe is not in the planets, or in the protons or neutrons, but in the *relationship between them.*"[12] The energy we call love flows between "God our Parent, God our Friend, and God our Holy Withness," who generously lavish that love on each of us.[13] This is what the Apostle John captured in the simple yet profound statement, "God is love."[14]

The triune God is a community sustained and energized by love. The power that flows between the Creator, Revealer, and Presence of Love is the same power unleashed in the creative process, whether galaxies are forming, cells are dividing, or relational brokenness is healing. It is "the power for infinite renewal,"[15] the "incomparably great power" that brings life from death.[16] It is the power Jesus

---

12. *The Divine Dance: The Trinity and Your Transformation,* Richard Rohr with Mike Morrell, pg. 56

13. Emily P. Freeman, The Soul Minimalist newsletter on Substack, 8/2/23

14. 1 John 4:8, NIV

15. *The Divine Dance: The Trinity and Your Transformation,* Richard Rohr with Mike Morrell, pg. 56

16. Ephesians 1:19, NIV

proclaimed when he said, "The kingdom of God has come near to you" as he healed physical and emotional wounds.[17]

This is the love that can never fail. It is always present, manifesting in myriad ways, relentlessly seeking restoration and reconciliation—seeking *shalom.*

Esteemed theologian Walter Brueggemann writes, "The central vision of world history in the Bible is that all of creation is one, every creature in community with every other, living in harmony and security toward the joy and well-being of every other creature."[18] It is a vision captured in the Trinity and the Great Commandment. Brueggemann asserts *shalom* is the word that conveys the vision.[19]

I appreciate Brueggemann's reflections on *shalom* because they are grounded in biblical texts that capture the complexity of life: "It is well-being that exists in the very midst of threats...in the very places where people always have to cope with anxiety, struggle for survival, and deal with temptation. It is well-being of a very personal kind...but it is also deliberately corporate."[20]

The God who is love, who offers a vision for abundant life characterized by *shalom*, is not a God who bypasses suffering but a God who offers to walk beside us, sharing the load. Jesus, whose path included Gesthemane and Golgotha, accompanies us on our journey to *shalom*. The invitation is open: "Come to me, all you who are weary and burdened, and I will give you rest. Take my yoke upon you and learn from me, for I am gentle and humble in heart, and you will find rest for your souls."[21]

Jesus offers companionship through the Spirit, who is our advocate. There is no shortcut on the journey to wholeness. While it's natural to long to be on the other side of challenges, I hope you will come to appreciate the beauty of this relational process as you connect with all of the tender and tough parts of you. What could be

---

17. Luke 10:9, NIV

18. *Living Toward a Vision: Biblical Reflections on Shalom,* Walter Brueggemann, pg. 15

19. Ibid, pg. 16

20. Ibid, pg. 16

21. Matthew 11:28-29, NIV

more worthy of your time than cultivating loving relationships—both internally and externally?

Living Toward the Vision

A compelling vision is essential for lasting change; a framework to guide that process is equally vital. Too often, in both secular and spiritual spaces, we cast a vision and exhort people to change without providing tangible, tested practices. This leads to discouragement and resignation. Techniques helpful to cope with a crisis or get through a difficult season might not support lasting change. Feeling stuck in patterns and cycles that recur despite significant effort is frustrating and demoralizing.

I want you to experience the freedom Jesus proclaimed when he announced his ministry. "The Spirit of the Lord is on me, because he has anointed me to proclaim good news to the poor. He has sent me to proclaim freedom for the prisoners and recovery of sight for the blind, to set the oppressed free, to proclaim the year of the Lord's favor."[22]

Reflect on these words with your new understanding of your internal family. Parts are constrained by the roles they adopted to survive, robbing them of vitality and blocking broader perspectives. Vulnerable, wounded parts are prisoners locked in the basement of the family home to contain their pain; cut off from healing resources, they can't see past their burdens. But there is good news! Through the power of love, we can free ourselves from painful emotions, distorted beliefs, and protective strategies provoked by fear of vulnerability.

Motivated by a vision of a mutually loving community—in ourselves, our relationships, and the world—transformation *is* possible. Healing happens. Abandoned exiles are restored. Weary protectors put down their shields, remove uniforms for jobs that are no longer needed, and reclaim their original purpose. Relationships plagued by shame and discord shift, and new possibilities emerge.

Healing happens because we increasingly lead our internal family with a harmonious blend of Self and Spirit. The most radical contribution of the IFS model—that everyone has a "Self," a leader with undamaged healing resources—is a profoundly biblical truth. Everyone bears God's image; we have God-given

---

22. Luke 4:18-19, NIV

resources no matter our life experiences. We reflect God's image—love—in tangible ways. Love manifests as curiosity, compassion, clarity, confidence, calm, creativity, connection, and courage. Love flows as the energy of the Spirit brings kindness, gentleness, faithfulness, and joy.

However, as we've explored, our God-given resources can be blocked or constrained. Wounds are inevitable; distressing experiences leave burdens of painful emotions and distorted beliefs that pose a risk to the inner system. Vulnerability provokes the fear that pain will overwhelm us, so burdened parts are exiled. Prisoners must have guards, so parts of us adopt protective roles such as criticizing, controlling, or caretaking to contain the pain. But pain can surface, prompting another group of protectors to rush in to numb or distract us.

As you interact with your internal family, you learn how much energy parts of you contain. Exiles are charged with the energy of painful emotions. When fear of vulnerability runs our lives, protectors who try to control everyone and everything lead. If their efforts fail, other protectors numb and distract us, and we miss out on our lives. Protectors are often at odds with one another, adding the energy of inner conflict. That is a *lot* of energy, and your body holds the exhaustion and tension of it. *Shalom*—wholeness, harmony, peace—often feels like an elusive ideal.

The commitment and effort required to live toward a vision of wholeness is significant. The challenging, complex, circuitous, and sometimes arduous process of healing can be daunting. But what will be lost if fear overrides love? What uniquely fascinating and compelling qualities of yours will remain hidden? What needs will go unnoticed or ignored? What bountiful energy will be wasted? What relationships will remain distant or disconnected? There is so much at stake.

Your heroic adventure is not a solo expedition. We all need community. You will increasingly feel the value of your inner community, and I hope you can also cultivate a community of others who share this understanding so you can support one another.

As you heal, your growth will inevitably impact others. The more we restore relationships within ourselves, the more we can be agents of reconciliation. Seeing others through a new lens helps us move beyond judgment to love.

My goal has been to equip you with a fresh vision for your journey and a user-friendly roadmap to support you each step of the way. I hope that, wherever you are in your healing process, you know you are Beloved and allow that truth to sustain you when the terrain is rugged and the light dims.

You are traveling an ancient path, reflected in the stories of God's people over the ages. Scripture repeatedly tells the story—on individual and communal levels—of intimacy marred by brokenness, followed by exile, then redemption and restoration through a loving relationship. God is inviting you—God's beloved—to journey from brokenness and exile to restoration, redemption, and reconciliation—to *shalom.* With the Spirit, the Self can restore relationships with protectors, earning their trust and gaining access to tender wounds. The presence of Self and Spirit creates a sacred space for welcoming the exiles, redeeming their suffering, and reconciling them with the rest of the inner family.

May you feel the incomparably great power of Love equipping and sustaining you on the road to wholeness.

Spiritual Practice: Meditating on God's Love

Reflect on the verses about love in 1 Corinthians through the lens of multiplicity, noticing the activity of different members of your inner family.

Love is patient; love is kind; love is not envious or boastful or arrogant or rude. It does not insist on its own way; it is not irritable or resentful; it does not rejoice in wrongdoing, but rejoices in the truth. It always protects, always trusts, always hopes, always perseveres. Love never fails.[23]

When you read what love is not, how does it shift your perspective to know that envy, boasting, arrogance, and rudeness are strategies protectors use to control or suppress pain? What if irritation and resentment are signals from parts of you that someone violated your boundaries—signals alerting you to their need for connection?

---

23. 1 Corinthians 13:4-8; NRSV except v. 7, NIV.

Releasing Constraints to Love

- Invite your internal family to join you in a meditation on the qualities of God's love.
- Breathe deeply, and exhale slowly. Visualize a sacred space filled with grace, a space safe enough for every part of you. If it's helpful, you can bring images to mind of the space—a scene from nature, a cozy room, etc.
- Picture yourself in the space, joined by every part of you that you've come to know in this journey.
- Imagine being surrounded and saturated by love that is patient and kind. There's no agenda for any part of you to be other than they are. They are welcome and loved.
- Feel the safety that fosters authenticity. What emotion arises as you are held by Love that is trustworthy?
- What hope do you have for healing? What issue, symptom, relationship, or dilemma do you want to offer to Love that never fails? Speak this need to the God who is Love.
- Invite your inner family members to breathe with you, taking in Love that meets every need and is always safe, trustworthy, patient, and kind. This is the Love of God with you now and always.

Re-read the verses and notice if there are strategies you resonate with, reflecting one of your protectors.

- Turn your attention to them, and notice how you feel toward them.
- If you aren't curious, confident, or compassionate, ask the other parts of you if they would be willing to step back.
- Now notice how you are feeling toward the original part.

- If you still don't feel Self-led, turn your attention to the part(s) of you who are blocking your heart.
    - Are you open to connecting with them?
    - If not, that's okay! Sometimes an issue provokes many parts of us, making our inner world confusing and chaotic. If that's the case, I encourage you to do the exercise above, inviting the specific parts you noticed to reflect on God's love.
- When you feel open to connecting with a part of you whose strategy echoes the verses—envy, boastful, rude, irritable, resentful, impatient, unkind—spend time with them to learn more about why they are doing their job.
    - How are you trying to help me?
    - What do you need from me?
    - What is it like for you to know you are not alone?
    - What are you afraid would happen if you stop doing what you're doing?
- If your protector shows you an exile, the part prompting their job, invite them into the sacred space where love flows. Do the above exercise with them, and notice how they respond.
- As always, I encourage you to use your journal to note your interactions with various inner family members.

Final Words of Encouragement

Imagining you reading these words touches my heart; you are motivated and hopeful enough about your healing to make it through this book! And that, my friend, is worth celebrating. Take a moment to acknowledge this step toward loving yourself, others, and God more freely.

Because you've taken in a lot of information and many new spiritual practices, I want to leave you with a simple reminder. The foundational spiritual practice is noticing your inner system with curiosity.

- Who is present today?
- How are they trying to help?
- What pain or discomfort lies below protective strategies?
- Is the Self leading in harmony with the Spirit, or are my God-given resources constrained?

Asking these questions and engaging with the parts you notice is transformative because you are listening. Your inner family members have stories to tell; patiently and persistently encouraging them to share reassures them they are not alone. Building relationships with them restores safety, trust, and hope.

As you meet the creative, courageous, and tenacious members of your internal family, consider this wisdom from Simone Weil. "Attention, taken to its highest degree, is the same thing as prayer. It presupposes faith and love."[24] May you be restored to wholeness as you attend to your internal family in faith and love.

24. I am indebted to Karen Swallow Prior for sharing this quote from Simone Weil's *Gravity and Grace,* pg. 117.

Acknowledgements

While writing is a solitary endeavor, the image I carry is of being at my desk energetically connected to the dear people who support my work. I am blessed to have had abundant encouragement from my "village" as this manuscript took shape.

When I showed a "draft of a draft" proposal for the project to Emily P. Freeman during our hope*writers mastermind retreat, her enthusiastic response provided fuel for the early months of traveling rabbit trails until the final form took shape.

Members of my writer's group—Reisha, Charissa, Sarah, Jean, and Jessica—never let me doubt that this work matters. Charissa took on the job of "first reader," bringing her expert eye and heartfelt response to each chapter. It is difficult to overstate how vital her partnership has been throughout the project.

As she did for my first book, Roxanne again took the time to review the manuscript. I sometimes joke that she is my "clone," with almost identical clinical training. Her IFS expertise and depth of experience with Scripture provided an ideal eye for detail.

As I contemplated potential editorial partners for the project, I learned that Jonathan Puddle, whose podcast and writing I admire, also works as an editor. I was delighted when he agreed to take on this project, and our work together confirmed my initial feeling that he was the perfect partner for this book.

I am indebted to Dr. Richard Schwartz for his willingness to listen to his clients' stories with humility. He allowed curiosity to lead, and the Internal Family Systems model took shape. Fortuitously, my training in IFS included three separate weeks of training with Dick and three years in his personal consultation group. Kind, brilliant, confident, and humble, Dick welcomed my work integrating IFS and Christian spirituality. My life and work have been transformed as a result of his mission to share IFS with the world.

Feedback from readers of my first book buoyed my confidence in the value of offering my perspective on the integration of IFS and Christian spirituality to the Christian community.

I am indebted to my clients, who are my greatest teachers. Their motivation to heal inspires me.

Final thanks go to my husband, who supports me in every endeavor, and my beloved children and grandchildren, who fill my life with joy.

About the Author

Molly LaCroix is a licensed marriage and family therapist specializing in treating the impact of trauma and adversity. She earned her master's degree in marriage and family therapy from Bethel Seminary San Diego, where she returned as an adjunct professor. She is a Level Three trained and Certified IFS therapist and IFS Clinical Consultant. Her first book, *Restoring Relationship: Transforming Fear into Love Through Connection*, helps readers identify and resolve barriers to loving themselves, others and God. She and her husband have two adult children who are married and parenting, and Molly's greatest joy is being Minnie to her grandchildren.

Learn more about Molly at mollylacroix.com.

instagram.com/mollylacroixlmft

facebook.com/MollyLaCroixLMFT

Also By Molly LaCroix

Available from Amazon.com

Printed in the USA
CPSIA information can be obtained
at www.ICGtesting.com
CBHW030454271223
2985CB00003B/34